THE LEGEND OF WERNER ENTERPRISES

JEFFREY L. RODENGEN
RICHARD F. HUBBARD

Edited by Heather Deeley
Design and layout by Rachelle Donley

Write Stuff Enterprises, Inc.
1001 South Andrews Avenue
Second Floor
Fort Lauderdale, FL 33316
1-800-900-Book (1-800-900-2665)
(954) 462-6657
www.writestuffbooks.com

Copyright © 2003 by Write Stuff Enterprises, Inc. All rights reserved. No part of this book may be reproduced or transmitted in any form by any means, electronic or mechanical, including photocopying and recording, or by any information storage or retrieval system, without permission in writing from the publisher.

Publisher's Cataloging in Publication

Rodengen, Jeffrey L.
　The legend of Werner Enterprises / Jeffrey L. Rodengen, Richard F. Hubbard ; edited by Heather Deeley; design and layout by Rachelle Donley—1st ed.
　p. cm.
　Includes bibliographical references and index.
　LCCN 20021150257
　ISBN 0-945903-94-4

　1. Werner Enterprises—History. 2. Trucking—United States—History. I. Hubbard, Richard F. II. Deeley, Heather III. Title

　HE5623.Z7W47 2003　　　388.3'24'06573
　　　　　　　　　　　　　QBI03-200836

Library of Congress
Catalog Card Number 20021150257

ISBN 0-945903-94-4

Completely produced in the
United States of America
10 9 8 7 6 5 4 3 2 1

Also by Jeffrey L. Rodengen

The Legend of Chris-Craft

*IRON FIST:
The Lives of Carl Kiekhaefer*

*Evinrude-Johnson
and The Legend of OMC*

*Serving the Silent Service:
The Legend of Electric Boat*

The Legend of Dr Pepper/Seven-Up

The Legend of Honeywell

The Legend of Briggs & Stratton

The Legend of Ingersoll-Rand

*The Legend of Stanley:
150 Years of The Stanley Works*

The MicroAge Way

The Legend of Halliburton

The Legend of York International

The Legend of Nucor Corporation

*The Legend of Goodyear:
The First 100 Years*

The Legend of AMP

The Legend of Cessna

The Legend of VF Corporation

The Spirit of AMD

The Legend of Rowan

*New Horizons:
The Story of Ashland Inc.*

The History of American Standard

The Legend of Mercury Marine

The Legend of Federal-Mogul

*Against the Odds:
Inter-Tel—The First 30 Years*

The Legend of Pfizer

*State of the Heart:
The Practical Guide to Your Heart
and Heart Surgery*
with Larry W. Stephenson, M.D.

*The Legend of
Worthington Industries*

The Legend of IBP, Inc.

*The Legend of
Trinity Industries, Inc.*

*The Legend of
Cornelius Vanderbilt Whitney*

The Legend of Amdahl

The Legend of Litton Industries

The Legend of Gulfstream

The Legend of Bertram
with David A. Patten

*The Legend of
Ritchie Bros. Auctioneers*

The Legend of ALLTEL
with David A. Patten

*The Yes, you can of
Invacare Corporation*
with Anthony L. Wall

*The Ship in the Balloon:
The Story of Boston Scientific
and the Development of
Less-Invasive Medicine*

The Legend of Day & Zimmermann

The Legend of Noble Drilling

*Fifty Years of Innovation:
Kulicke & Soffa*

*Biomet—From Warsaw
to the World*
with Richard F. Hubbard

NRA: An American Legend

*The Heritage and Values
of RPM, Inc.*

*The Marmon Group:
The First Fifty Years*

The Legend of Grainger

*The Legend of
The Titan Corporation*
with Richard F. Hubbard

The Legend of Discount Tire Co.
with Richard F. Hubbard

The Legend of Polaris
with Richard F. Hubbard

The Legend of La-Z-Boy
with Richard F. Hubbard

The Legend of McCarthy
with Richard F. Hubbard

*InterVoice:
Twenty Years of Innovation*
with Richard F. Hubbard

*Jefferson-Pilot Financial:
A Century of Excellence*
with Richard F. Hubbard

The Legend of HCA
with Richard F. Hubbard

TABLE OF CONTENTS

Foreword by Roger Penske vi

Acknowledgments viii

Chapter I	Birth of the Trucking Industry	10
Chapter II	The Long Haul Begins	24
Chapter III	Building the Werner Family	34
Chapter IV	Full Speed Ahead	44
Chapter V	The Brave New World of Trucking	56
Chapter VI	Werner Goes Public	66
Chapter VII	Traveling a Bumpy Road	76
Chapter VIII	Information Highway	90
Chapter IX	Crossing Borders	106
Chapter X	For the Long Haul	122

Notes to Sources 140

Index 146

Foreword

BY
Roger Penske
Founder of Penske Corporation

© 2003 EXLEY-FOTO, INC.

America, with smooth interstates and wide open spaces, is a trucker's dream. We all depend on trucks to move everything from auto parts to zucchini from coast to coast. However, the trucking industry has had anything but a smooth ride.

The early years in the business for Werner Enterprises Chairman C. L. Werner were extraordinarily challenging. But those same struggles forged a remarkable vision and work ethic that would transport Werner Enterprises to the very top of the trucking industry. Forced by regulation to compete against all odds and much larger and more established companies, C. L. was determined to make Werner Enterprises the best and most reliable trucking firm possible.

As the founder of Penske Corporation, a transportation services company, I was immediately impressed by C. L. when I first met him. In 1988 my company had just acquired Detroit Diesel from General Motors, and I was very interested in meeting the top movers and shakers in the over-the-road trucking industry. Werner Enterprises was a marquee account in that business, and I had the privilege to visit one evening with C. L. and his sons. I knew immediately that the Werners were a group we could work with. From that meeting, we forged a world-class relationship between our two organizations—a deep relationship of trust.

Among the attributes that have always set the Werners apart was their commitment to both customers and to technology. For them, the two are inseparable. C. L. and his sons are extremely knowledgeable about the technical aspects of engines. I'll never forget that first meeting so many years ago. When everyone in the industry was using mechanically fueled engines, Detroit Diesel introduced a new Series 60 that was really the first electronic, four-cycle, six-cylinder engine, and Werner Enterprises was one of the very first fleets to adopt it. The engine had all the attributes of the next generation—fuel injection, overhead camshaft, advanced diagnostics, automatic overspeed shutdown, and an opportunity to review information if there had been an accident. C. L. and his sons grilled me on the benefits of the engine's fuel economy, reliability, maintainability, and emissions. More importantly, they made me aware that they wanted the engine that scored the best in each category so they could ensure that Werner customers received the very best service, the highest reliability, and the most favorable pricing. Further, Werner's trucks turned out to be worth more at resale or trade-in time with our engines than they did with a Cat or a Cummins, and that was a huge, huge benefit for both of us. After that meeting I had something much more valuable and much more durable than a thick contract—I had C. L.'s word. We had a handshake, and we never looked back.

I have also been sincerely impressed with how the Werner family has worked together as a highly effective and integrated team. Having four sons and a daughter myself—two of whom are in the business with me—I know how hard it can be to separate family and business, to delineate responsibilities to your children, to help them grow within the organization, and to teach them the leadership qualities that will earn the respect of those who work for them. I think C. L. has done an absolutely outstanding job of that. I know it's tough to work for a father who has been successful, but each of C. L.'s sons has continued to strengthen the solid culture and rock-solid foundation that C. L. established for Werner Enterprises.

Since federal deregulation in 1980, the trucking industry has been among the most competitive and capital-intensive industries in America. Hundreds of both established and potential competitors have coasted down the financial off-ramp to obscurity and bankruptcy. What then sets Werner Enterprises apart from the rest? First and foremost has been the Werner commitment to its legion of satisfied customers. By employing the very latest in technology both on and off the road Werner has left its competition miles behind. The first and only company to employ a paperless log system, Werner has made its drivers among the most efficient on the road. Its data processing and scheduling systems are the most advanced in the industry—in fact, in most industries—and its satellite location and two-way communications systems are the envy of the trucking world.

It's not surprising then that Werner was one of the pioneers in the industry to go public and to be listed on the Nasdaq Stock Exchange. But even though Werner shares have enjoyed a remarkable record of earnings and market capitalization, the Werners have managed to run the business with an entrepreneurial zeal that has disappeared in so many large corporations today. Hard as it is to imagine, Werner Enterprises remains the tenacious, hands-on, family-like company of its early days. I'm proud to have been associated with this truly American success story, and the opportunity to share my thoughts is a true honor.

Racing legend Roger Penske is one of the best-known and most successful car and track owners in the history of motor sports. He is founder and chairman of Penske Corporation, a transportation services company that includes Penske Truck Leasing, Penske Automotive Group, UnitedAuto Group, Transportation Resource Partners, Penske Transportation Components, and Penske Performance. Penske Corporation and its subsidiaries manage and operate businesses with annual revenues of approximately $12 billion and 35,000 employees at more than 1,700 locations worldwide.

With over 45 years of racing experience, Penske has built one of the most successful empires in the sports world while setting almost every record in racing. Penske Racing, Inc., is the most successful Indy racing team in history, boasting 119 wins, highlighted by a record 13 Indianapolis 500 victories, 11 National Championships, and 144 pole positions. Penske Racing also has more than 50 victories in the NASCAR Winston Cup Series.

In 1988 Penske bought the ailing Detroit Diesel, a manufacturer of heavy-duty diesel and alternative fuel engines, and within 10 years tripled Detroit Diesel's sales.

ACKNOWLEDGMENTS

A GREAT NUMBER OF people assisted in the research, preparation, and publication of *The Legend of Werner Enterprises*.

Research assistant Patrick LaGreca helped compile the archival research and composed the first narrative time line. Heather Deeley, associate editor, oversaw the text and photos from beginning to end. Art Director Rachelle Donley's graphic design brought the story to vivid life.

Special thanks are due to the Werners themselves. Founder, Chairman, and CEO C. L. Werner; Vice Chairman Gary Werner; President and COO Greg Werner; Vice Chairman of Corporate Development Curt Werner; and attorney Gail Werner-Robertson generously shared their time and memories.

This book would not have been possible without the invaluable assistance by Werner executive assistants Grace O'Connell and Stefanie Nelsen, who served as our liaisons; advertising supervisor Lisa Fairbairn, who provided us with photos; and Executive Vice President and General Counsel Richard Reiser, whose attention to detail kept things moving smoothly.

Many Werner team members, retirees, friends, and associates greatly enriched the book by discussing their experiences. The authors extend particular gratitude to these men and women for their candid recollections and anecdotes: Duane Acklie, Al Adams, Don Bacon, Jim Belter, Donald Broughton, Wayne Childers, Cecil and Sharon Curry, Dan Cushman, Randy Dickerson, Jeff Doll, Lee Easton, Jerry Ehrlich, Irving Epstein, Marcella Ernst, J. D. Farris, Steve Finnes, Paul Finney, Rod French, John Frey, Gerald Hanks, Gene Hansohn, Dwayne Haug, Lee Hays, Jim Hebe, August "Ben" Hein, Conrad Heinson, Duane Henn, Donna Johnson, Jim Johnson, John Keenan, Jim Larson, Derek Leathers, Bill Legg, Paul Mecray, Marty Nordlund, Larry Olson, Patricia Packett, Buddy Payton, Dick Pierson, Mark Pigott, Jack Platt, Scott Reed, Scott Robertson, Don Rogert, Dean Sapp,

Wilbur Smith, John Steele, Bob Synowicki, Martin Thompson, Gerald Timmerman, Guy Welton, Gale Wickersham, Larry Williams, and Sue Witherell.

As always, special thanks are extended to the dedicated staff at Write Stuff Enterprises, Inc.: Jon VanZile, executive editor; Melody Maysonet, senior editor; Bonnie Freeman and Kevin Allen, copy editors; Mary Aaron, transcriptionist; Barbara Koch, indexer; Sandy Cruz, senior art director; Dennis Shockley, art director; Bruce Borich, production manager; Marianne Roberts, vice president of administration; Sherry Hasso, bookkeeper; Linda Edell, executive assistant to Jeffrey L. Rodengen; Lars Jessen, director of worldwide marketing; and Irena Xanthos, sales and promotions manager.

A family drove this GMC truck via the National Park Highway from Seattle to New York in 31 days as part of a company-sponsored promotional journey in 1916. *(Photo courtesy of The National Automotive History Collection [NAHC])*

Birth of the Trucking Industry
1900–1955

Life is either a daring adventure or nothing.

—Helen Keller

IN THE 19TH CENTURY, THE vastness of the New World was astounding to its settlers of European ancestry. But with the promise of unlimited space came the reality of isolation. Although individual communities were generally able to subsist on their own, the demand for difficult-to-obtain goods and services grew. Improved transportation was becoming a necessity. Not only would it have the capacity to move goods and people from place to place; it also was needed to carry an ever increasing flow of information.

Hubs and Spokes

Railroads in the United States linked the East and West Coasts in 1869, and the largest inland communities sprang up close to the main rail lines. By the end of the century, much of the inland settlement was complete, and the railroads had branched into areas beyond the trunk lines.

The railroad system began an extensive rebuilding around 1896 due to a boom in the economy. As quickly as the railroad progressed, it barely kept up with the increasing demands of a spreading population. The railroads desperately needed a subsystem more sophisticated than horse and wagon. They needed branches on their branches.

Around the same time, other forms of transportation were being introduced. "Horseless carriages," or automobiles, made their appearance at the turn of the century. Although the early cars were often unreliable, city fathers envisioned the future and began to pave roads, and by the early 1900s, many cities bustled with electric automobiles delivering staple items.[1]

The first gasoline truck was produced in 1896 at the Daimler Benz factory in Germany. By the end of the century, the company was turning out trucks capable of carrying a five-ton payload.[2] Initially these trucks did not make much of an impression in the U.S. market, where the steam engine was the workhorse of industrial labor. Using technology borrowed from the railroads, the fire departments played a notable role in the steam engine's adaptation for vehicles. Originally the engines were used to power only the pumps, and horsepower still transported the rig.

Fire equipment companies such as Ward La France didn't take long to realize that the entire vehicle could run much faster using steam-generated power, however. The technology then made its way into farm equipment such as steam-powered threshing and harvesting machines.[3]

Swiss manufacturer Saurer superceded Mack Brothers when it introduced five-ton, gasoline-powered trucks in the early 1900s. Above is a circa 1911 example. *(Photo courtesy of NAHC)*

Gasoline engine fire trucks, such as this 1908 Olds model, began replacing steam engine models as early as 1905. *(Photo courtesy of NAHC)*

The manufacture and sale of steam trucks soon was eclipsed by the arrival of the more reliable gasoline-powered trucks. A number of these vehicles were on the market as early as 1905.[4]

The Rewards of Healthy Competition

In 1903 Mack Brothers Company introduced a four-cylinder, gasoline-powered bus, which was soon overshadowed by the Swiss company Saurer's five-ton trucks. In 1905 both Mack and Studebaker battled

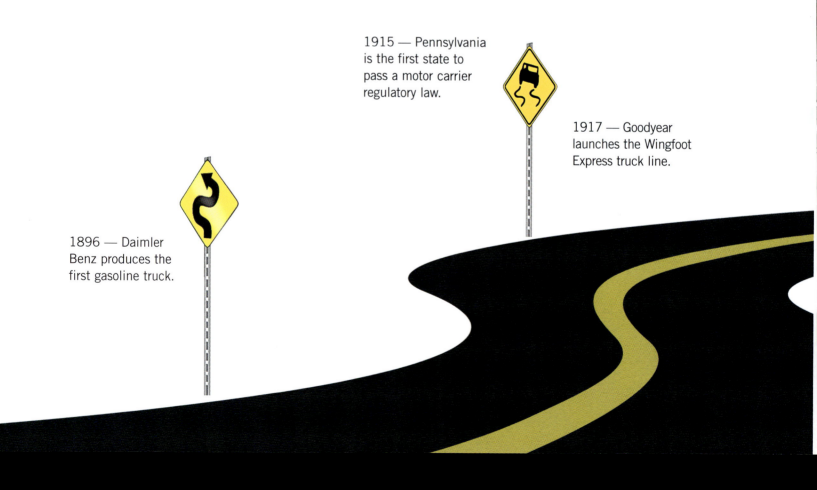

1915 — Pennsylvania is the first state to pass a motor carrier regulatory law.

1917 — Goodyear launches the Wingfoot Express truck line.

1896 — Daimler Benz produces the first gasoline truck.

CHAPTER ONE: BIRTH OF THE TRUCKING INDUSTRY

back with the introduction of their own five-ton trucks.[5]

These early vehicles were a far cry from today's user-friendly models. In fact, the driver was the last thing early manufacturers took into consideration. There were no cabs, just a bench above the front axle and a steering column protruding between the driver's legs. The vehicles had springs, but they served to cushion the load, not the driver. The wheels were adapted from carriages and consisted of simply a steel rim surrounded by a hard rubber strip.[6]

Mack quickly made innovations to stay ahead of the competition. In its New York factory, Mack was the first to standardize truck production. It introduced dual rear tires well ahead of their time. Mack also added a much thicker rubber strip to the tires for greater durability and heavy-duty workloads.[7]

Reliance, the heavy-duty model of the GMC line, entered the market in 1905. This circa 1909 vehicle is an early example of a truck with a cab. *(Photo courtesy of NAHC)*

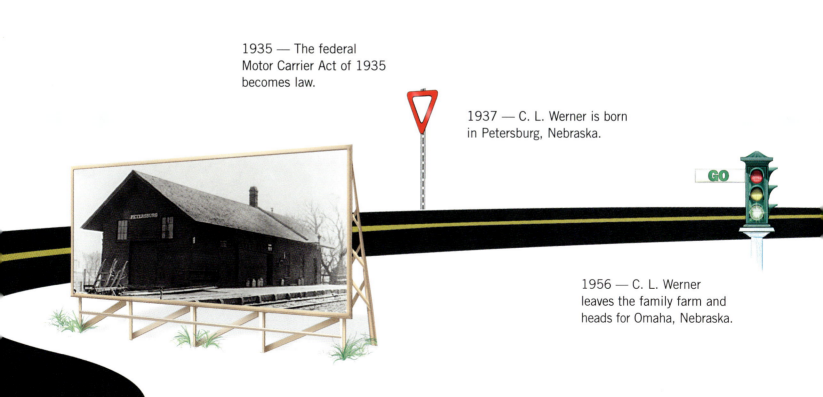

1935 — The federal Motor Carrier Act of 1935 becomes law.

1937 — C. L. Werner is born in Petersburg, Nebraska.

1956 — C. L. Werner leaves the family farm and heads for Omaha, Nebraska.

Other truck manufacturers made their debut in the early 1900s. International Harvester was perhaps the first company to recognize and take advantage of the booming agricultural market. By 1909 the White brothers began building gasoline trucks. During that time, both Rapid Motor Vehicles and Reliance Motor Truck entered the market.[8]

Below: A circa 1910 five-ton White Company truck. White began producing gasoline trucks in 1909.

Opposite: Rapid, maker of this circa 1911 one-ton tour vehicle, later joined with GMC's Reliance. The Rapid and Reliance names were then dropped in favor of the GMC trademark. *(Photos courtesy of NAHC)*

As technology advanced, competition kept pace. Companies began to sponsor impressive exhibitions, such as transcontinental journeys, to promote their products. In 1916, a couple and their child drove from Seattle to New York in 31 days in a GMC truck. Their route was the National Park Highway, then only a series of strung-together dirt roads.[9]

The Wingfoot Express

Goodyear Tire & Rubber followed GMC with a similar marketing ploy in 1917. Solid tires minimized speed, provided a rough ride, and kept gasoline mileage to a minimum. Goodyear developed its pneumatic, or "air cushioned," tire to increase vehicle speed and durability. The tire was much better at absorbing treacherous road conditions while providing nonskid properties that made it easier for vehicles to climb up and down steep hills. The company believed pneumatic tires could make trucks more valuable than railways for hauling goods, opening a vast market for tires.[10]

To sell this concept, Goodyear developed a special truck line, the Wingfoot Express, a five-ton Packard truck fitted with 38-by-7-inch front and 44-by-10-inch rear cord tires, departing Akron, Ohio, for Boston.[11] Due to bad roads and worse weather, that first trip took 19 days. Equipped with the first sleepers, the Wingfoot Express fleet was soon making the round-trip in five days, faster than train travel. One month after the first Wingfoot Express made the historic trip from Akron to Boston, Goodyear President Frank Sieberling announced to the U.S. Chamber of Commerce,

THE STRAIGHT STORY

THE FIRST AUTO TIRES MADE DRIVING a tricky business. The smooth tread of what were essentially overgrown bike tires skidded and lasted only about 2,000 miles. The industry standard was the pneumatic Clincher tire, invented by Thomas Jeffery. It featured a rubber bead—the part that holds the tire to the rim—that required a crowbar "and a bit of profanity" to stretch for mounting and demounting.[1]

Because the tires wore out so quickly, car owners grew frustrated with the time and energy required to change them. Horse lovers and naysayers claimed this inconvenience would destroy the automobile's success. A better tire was needed, and the three biggest companies of the day—U.S. Rubber, B. F. Goodrich, and Diamond—concentrated on perfecting the Clincher's design.[2] But Goodyear's management team had never liked the Clincher and began working on a different design as early as 1900, when auto registrations totaled just over 4,000.[3]

Goodyear's first innovation was the addition of a braided piano wire to the tire's bead. The wire was then cured into the bead, which held the tire onto the rim with a complicated set of locks. Since the tire didn't curve to fit the rim, as

---

"The introduction of the motor truck into our commercial life sounds the death knell of the short-line railroad."[12]

The following year, Goodyear launched the nation's first transcontinental truck line. On September 1, 1918, two large trucks left Boston, arriving in San Francisco on September 22.[13] Each truck had two drivers. While one drove, the other slept behind the driver's seat. The actual ride time for the 3,700-mile trip was 289 hours, an average of nearly 13 miles per hour. Travel was slowed by poor trails over mountains and by rotted bridges, some of which had to be rebuilt hastily to get the trucks across rushing streams.[14] More than 70 percent of the roads were unpaved, not only proving the quality of Goodyear's tires, but also making the case for the viability of truck transportation. In 1926 Goodyear retired the Wingfoot Express, but the pneumatic tire had caught on with a vengeance.

Meanwhile on the West Coast, a company called Gersix, in Portland, Oregon, fathered the idea of building custom trucks. These vehicles sported a six-cylinder engine with full electrical equipment. Their manufacture time was one month, and they sold for about twice the price of a factory truck. Gersix went on to become Kenworth and would carry the custom truck tradition into the next millennium.[15]

World War I

On April 6, 1917, with Great Britain and France on the verge of collapse in their war against Germany and its allies, the United States abandoned its position of neutrality and entered World War I. As costly and devastating as the war would be, many American businesses grew as a result of the war effort, and the trucking industry was no exception. Governments spent millions of dollars to manufacture trucks and research ways to increase their size and durability.[16]

By 1917 most major railroads were bankrupt, but not because of competition from trucking. In 1910, the federal government had removed the railroads' right to regulate prices, preventing them from recouping renovation investments and reinvesting in the industry.[17] This burden on the railroads combined with the war effort to create a fertile environment for a trucking industry.

During the war, domestic demand for trucks to transport food and construction materials rose to an all-time high. Also, the Allied Forces had plenty of uses for rugged vehicles overseas.[18] The Mack AC, for example, had a steel cab—a first—and an optional roof. It quickly became the champion truck of the wartime effort. The British troops, noting the ferocious look of the vehicle's front end, dubbed it "The Bulldog Mack,"

the Clincher did, it could hold 10 percent more compressed air, providing a more comfortable ride. Goodyear named the tire the Straight Side.[4]

A significant breakthrough, the Straight Side was still prone to blowouts. In 1903, Goodyear created a design with improved resiliency.[5] The new tire featured an open-weave fabric between the tread and the tire carcass. The fabric would "rivet" these components together during vulcanization (the chemical treatment that makes rubber stronger and more elastic) by allowing the rubber to flow through the weave.[6] The tire was held on by a metal locking device and required a new kind of rim. Thus the Universal Rim was born, able to fit either a Clincher or the new lock-on Straight Side.[7]

The Straight Side pneumatic tire didn't revolutionize the automobile industry overnight and took even longer to edge its way into the truck market. It first underwent a transformation by the Palmer Tire Company in England. Palmer developed a tire called the Silvertown that used woven cords bound by thin crosshairs to reduce tearing of the standard square-woven fabric.[8]

In response, Goodyear developed a fabric with cords slightly thicker than the square-weave, but held together by cross threads so fine they broke during vulcanization, thus eliminating chafing, which weakened the tire.[9] Conceived in 1912, this development led in 1916 to a pneumatic tire durable enough for truck use. It was featured in Goodyear's Wingfoot Express marketing campaign and its ensuing transcontinental truck line.

prompting Mack to adopt the bulldog as its company icon shortly thereafter.[19]

Roads accordingly assumed new importance. At the turn of the century, less than 200 miles of hard-surfaced highway sliced through the rural United States. It wasn't until 1916, with car registrations topping 1.5 million nationwide, that the Federal Aid Road Act appropriated $75 million to build rural roads.[20] The completion of the Lincoln Highway was a major triumph. In 1919 it carried future President Dwight Eisenhower's Transcontinental Army convoy from the nation's capital to San Francisco. According to a 1921 Chamber of Commerce report, the Road Act money was used to "connect practically every city and town of 5,000 or more inhabitants in the United States" so that almost 90 percent of the nation's population would live within 10 miles of a Federal Aid Road.[21] By the late 1920s nearly half a million miles of surfaced road covered the United States.[22]

Like railroads, the trucking industry struggled with regulation. In 1915, Pennsylvania became the first state to pass a motor carrier regulatory law. By 1923, 19 states had each adopted their own version.[23] The result was pandemonium.

The basic objective of most of the state laws was to tax interstate carriers and subject them to safety regulations. Some states attempted to discriminate between contract carriers (carrying a specific company's goods) and common carriers (carrying the goods of different companies), but most of these double standards were struck down by the courts.[24]

The Great Depression—The Industry Maker

The trucking industry was about to receive its greatest boost yet, but it came during a harrowing economic time for the nation. On October 24, 1929, a wave of panic engulfed dazed brokers, investors, and bankers on Wall Street as the stock market plummeted to unprecedented and spectacular losses. Within an hour during the frantic day, blue-chip stocks of companies such as General Electric, Johns-Manville, and Montgomery Ward tumbled, in some cases losing 25 percent of their value.

As the American economy went into a tailspin, the budding trucking industry supplied feed, grain, flour, and food. While prices of almost all goods fell, the demand to move them on a moment's notice remained.

The Depression forced the typical American business to operate on a shoestring budget. Decisions were based no longer on profit maximization but on fear and survival. Manufacturing supplies were purchased on an as-needed basis, and production was limited to immediate orders. Cost per unit went up, and margins went down, but the nation still had to eat. The nature of the trucking service allowed it to adopt what would become known as customer focus. In short, the trucking industry was more capable of customizing services than any other shipping method.

In 1929 the total freight transported in the United States by all methods added up to 744 billion ton-miles. In 1932 that tonnage dropped to a Depression-era low of 453 billion ton-miles. During the same period, the trucking industry increased its share of the load from 18.2 billion to 23.7 billion ton-miles. In other words, as the transportation industry as a whole shrank by nearly 40 percent, trucking grew by more than 30 percent.[25]

But growing market share was only part of the story. During this time, the trucking industry had also taken on the transportation of higher-valued goods. Due to the risk involved with this type of cargo, carriers could charge substantially higher fees. Consequently, as the trucking industry proved itself in its new, higher-end market, its revenues took a leap.[26]

As unemployment grew, many people looked for new ways to feed their families. The barriers to entry into the trucking business were low, so many people "bet the farm" on the success of their trucking endeavor. As competition grew more heated, the temptation to resort to underhanded business practices sometimes became irresistible. Though many practices were not technically illegal under the loose tangle of state statutes, the industry's reputation began to suffer.

Hours worked by the drivers became one of the major problems. With the economy so weak and margins so low, truckers found it extremely difficult to earn a living wage, even with increased demand and sometimes higher fees. Thus it was not uncommon for drivers to travel for stretches of 20 hours or more in an attempt to produce or increase profits. The result was higher safety risk, not only for truckers but also for anyone else using the roadways. This practice of overworking drivers, though born of the Depression, would persist and grow in years to come.[27]

The Federal Motor Carrier Act of 1935

In 1933, to boost the industry's integrity and standards, Congress passed the National Industrial Recovery Act, setting forth voluntary industry codes on wages, maximum hours worked, and even rates.[28] The Act was by and large a failure, but it smoothed the way for further federal regulation. The American Trucking Association (ATA), the most powerful trade association at the time, was beginning to solidify, and although few embraced full-scale regulation, most members understood that some action had to be taken to correct the widespread abuses.[29]

President Franklin D. Roosevelt had appointed Joseph B. Eastman federal coordinator of transportation in 1933, hoping to get a handle on the trucking situation. It didn't take Eastman long to call for federal legislation. The ATA strongly backed his recommendation, and the Motor Carrier Act of 1935 became law. Its first declaration was to place the regulation of motor carriers under the jurisdiction of the Interstate Commerce Commission (ICC).[30]

Although the ATA had initially supported the bill, the industry soon had some mixed emotions. The small trucker felt the bill favored larger carriers. Many carriers felt the bill limited competition between truckers and the railroads. Yet most agreed that the law benefited legitimate transportation business and that the only ones who would really suffer would be the dishonest elements the bill was intended to purge.[31]

The provisions of the federal Motor Carrier Act were spelled out in detail. The most significant required that a common carrier receive a certificate of "public convenience and necessity." Essentially, a company was required to prove it was the best carrier for a particular job based on convenience and necessity to the public. But confusion was sparked by a grandfather clause allowing companies to argue they had been performing these services all along and thus should maintain the rights. The ICC became inundated with applications and counterclaims, and by 1937 it had issued only 1,088 permits out of some 51,000 applications. It wasn't until nearly 1940 that the ICC would begin to catch up with its backlog.[32]

GROWING PAINS

COMMERCIALLY, RAILROADS DID NOT function in the same way as highways. The roadways of the early 1900s were subject to a flat tax. Thus, if a farmer wanted to deliver grain, he paid a toll to compensate for the distance. The farmer also paid a carrier. With railroads, however, the carrier owned both the means of transportation and the roadway on which it traveled. The railroads had invested enormous capital in the development and maintenance of this system, and since they were a monopoly, they had no motivation to keep costs down. High prices made access to rail transportation difficult for many American businesses to obtain and inevitably provoked an outcry for regulation.[1]

Because each state had the power to legislate and govern itself as the residents saw fit, each state regulated the railroads independently. Some states enacted more stringent laws than others. Some passed no legislation. Companies tended to migrate to railroad-friendly states.[2]

In 1886 the U.S. Supreme Court overturned an Illinois law that regulated railroad rates, holding that only Congress could regulate interstate commerce.[3] The Interstate Commerce Act (ICA) of 1887 eliminated or exposed various corrupt practices and required railroads not only to publish rates but to post them everywhere that railroads conducted business.[4] As far as the rates themselves were concerned, Congress opted for a "reasonable and just" limitation to avoid any government interference in the free market. Additionally, the act created the Interstate Commerce Commission (ICC) to handle disputes between railroad and client, thus creating the first federal regulatory agency.[5]

The authority of the ICC was initially so vague that it had no real means of enforcement; it became so inundated with grievances that many cases took as long as four years to address—and most ICC rulings were overturned in court. Despite having to deal with this bureaucracy, the railroads continued to thrive.[6]

The federal Motor Carrier Act held carriers to seven basic rules:

1. Publication and observance of reasonable and nondiscriminatory rates
2. ICC discretionary power to set maximum and minimum rates and to suspend a proposed carrier rate for a maximum of seven months
3. Adequate insurance for public liability, property damage, and cargo loss and damage
4. ICC approval of security issues of more than $500,000 and all consolidations, mergers, and purchases
5. Regulation of employee qualifications and maximum work hours
6. Adherence to equipment and safety-of-operation standards
7. Uniform accounting and periodic reporting of operating and financial statistics[33]

Most notable were the new restraints regarding hours worked by drivers. They trimmed the voluntary guidelines by prohibiting an operator from driving more than 10 hours in a 24-hour period without eight consecutive hours of down time. Additionally, a driver was not to exceed 60 hours of on duty time in a week or 70 hours in a 192-hour period.[34]

Many of these provisions were virtually unenforceable. In the long run, the government stepped in with nationwide rules that are still evolving today.

World War II and the Next Leap

The Depression shaped truck manufacturing as it did the rest of the economy: Technological advances slowed. Then on December 7, 1941, more than 360 Japanese warplanes swarmed down on the United States Navy in Pearl Harbor, Hawaii. More than 2,000 navy personnel perished, along with 400 civilians. Five U.S. battleships and 14 smaller ships were sunk or seriously damaged. President Roosevelt called the attack "a brilliant feat of deception, perfectly timed and executed with great skill." Within days, the United States would declare war on Japan, Italy, and Germany and join the horrible fury of world war.

Before the Pearl Harbor attack, only 2.5 percent of Americans favored United States involvement in the European conflict.[35] American industry, however, was already preparing to help Great Britain. In 1940 President Roosevelt asked Congress for $1.9 billion in defense. Later that year, Congress approved $17 billion. In essence, the money for "defense," or "national interest," was marked for industry; it was apparent to many that the conflict with Germany must be won in American factories, and by 1941 the United States had begun an immense defensive buildup. Then Pearl Harbor jolted the war effort into full swing.

American ingenuity skyrocketed. Automobile and truck manufacturers quickly converted their facilities to produce combat vehicles and mechanical parts. Between 1939 and 1945, U.S. truck manufacturers built and shipped nearly 150,000 heavy-class trucks and 3 million soft-skinned vehicles, not including tanks. At home, orders for domestic vehicles would have to wait.[36]

Once again, rubber restrictions were imposed. The shortage was compounded by Japan's seizing South Pacific rubber plantations recently developed by American companies. In an effort to meet domestic demand, Goodyear introduced a passenger car tire made of regenerated rubber. American industry adopted the slogan "Keep 'em rolling," referring to the at-home effort to support the troops overseas.[37]

During the war, the country as a whole suffered a manpower shortage, and the trucking industry was not immune. Drivers were recruited from all walks of life. Women became drivers, older men came out of retirement, and boys learned to drive rigs. The influx of inexperienced personnel caused a rise in accidents and mishaps, one of many prices paid so that industry could keep up with wartime demand.[38]

More and more on America's roads, "store-to-door" delivery was turning into "war-plant-to-arsenal" delivery, and the trucks were carrying military matériel.[39]

In 1940 the government had established a Department of Transportation (DOT) to plan in case war ensued. Unfortunately, DOT was unaware of many post–World War I changes in the trucking industry. Its shortsightedness created the need for a new transportation agency, and in 1941 President Roosevelt created the Office of Defense Transportation (ODT) and appointed ICC Chairman Joseph B. Eastman its head.[40]

Trucking issues virtually consumed the ODT. Due to the national emergency, the ODT had to act quickly and forcibly in many instances. It forced companies to give up parallel routes and asked the 48 states to adopt a 40-mile-per-hour speed limit to conserve fuel and rubber. (Only 11 states complied.) Perhaps the most relevant issue it addressed was the restriction of interstate transportation. Even after the ICC came along, states kept enforcing their laws restricting out-of-state carriers. The ODT asked the 48 governors for a moratorium on these restrictions, and every state adopted the ODT's guideline. The states revived their restrictions after the war, but the moratorium had set a precedent for uniform laws.[41]

During the war, many companies retooled to manufacture arms and aircraft. The resulting expertise in turn enriched the trucking industry, among others. In 1941, Cummins installed the world's first aluminum diesel engine in a Kenworth truck, and three years later, the first extruded aluminum frame.[42] Both innovations represented significant advances toward the next generation of lighter, more efficient trucks. Other by-products of war work included adjustable seats and heaters that worked without asphyxiating drivers. These amenities seemed remarkable at the time and would later give birth to the modern luxury cab.

Opposite: Civilian trucks evolved into military trucks. This World War II 2.5-ton-payload GMC was dubbed the "Jimmy" and the "deuce and a half." *(Photo courtesy of NAHC)*

Postwar Struggles

The years immediately following the war's end in 1945 were not the trucking industry's best. Highways were in poor condition and needed rebuilding, and the postwar "era of good feeling" put more cars on the road than anyone had ever imagined. In 1951, registered passenger cars totaled 39.5 million, an increase of more than 10 million in 10 years. Truck registration had nearly doubled during the same period, reaching 8.5 million in 1951.[43] Nonprofessional drivers, some of whom were first-time drivers and intimidated by the big rigs' size, blamed the road conditions on the trucks. The motor carrier industry desperately needed a public relations campaign.[44]

In the nick of time, the Mack Brothers Company produced a vacuum-assisted auxiliary transmission, enabling drivers to shift with one hand. Coupled with a new diesel engine, the new transmission helped launch the industry's next era. Mack took the rig on a road show—not so much to sell the truck to the industry as to sell the industry to the public. The company appealed to Americans' love of anything modern and convinced them that modern trucks—not antiquated trains—would be the way goods were delivered in America.[45]

Still, the postwar years took a toll on the trucking industry. Many companies that once flourished were unable to compete. Companies sold and

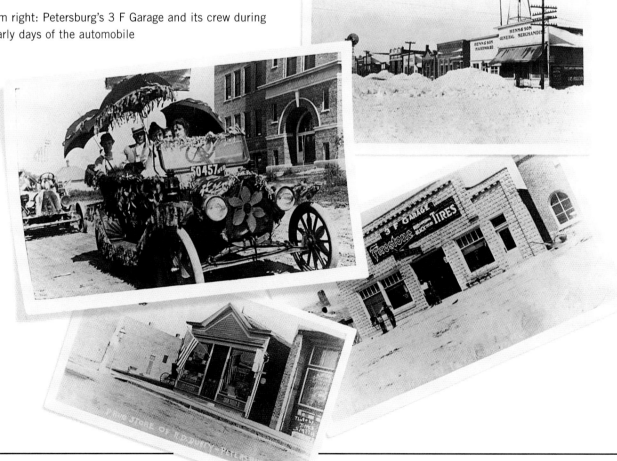

Below left: A parade through the streets of Petersburg, Nebraska. In the background is C. L. Werner's childhood school, St. John's.

Bottom left: The R. D. Duffy Drug Store, in Petersburg, in the mid-1930s

Right: Main Street after a snowstorm in Petersburg during the 1930s—testimony to the harsh winters on the Great Plains

Bottom right: Petersburg's 3 F Garage and its crew during the early days of the automobile

merged on a regular basis. Long gone, it seemed, were the days when a savvy entrepreneur could obtain a truck and, through hard work, build and live the American dream. By the 1950s the barriers confronting a start-up trucking company seemed too high and too risky. But a young man named Clarence "C. L." Werner would not be deterred.

An Industry Leader Is Born

C. L. was born in May 1937 in Petersburg, Nebraska, a small farm town in Boone County about 150 miles northwest of Omaha. This was America's heartland, and during the 1930s it would be difficult to say which took a greater toll on the area—the Great Depression or the dust bowl.

In those days, doctors still came to farms to deliver babies. So it was with infant C. L., the third of seven children born into the Werner family. Large families were critical to the survival of farms, but they also meant more mouths to feed. And during those lean years in America, keeping everyone fed was objective number one.[46]

"Those were the tough old days," C. L. said. "We heated the main part of the house in the daytime with wood and coal and went without heat altogether at night. It wasn't a well-constructed or well-insulated house. Sometimes in the morning, there would be snow on our blankets that had blown through the cracks around the windows."[47]

The Werner children were up at 5 A.M. to start their daily chores, then rode a horse and buggy to school. "We were very young, but we were responsible enough to hook up our buggy and put our horse in the school's barn," he recalled. "It was a Catholic school, and all our teachers were nuns. They were tough on us, but I'm glad. If I ever got popped, I deserved it. In fact, I probably deserved a hell of a lot more than I got."[48]

After school, the Werner children resumed their chores on the 160 acres of land. Crops were grown largely to feed livestock. The sale of milk, cream, eggs, and livestock generated most of the income. Rarely was there excess grain to sell. "We'd milk about 20 cows by hand and take care of the livestock—30 or 40 head of cattle, maybe 100 porkers, and my mother always had 300 to 400 chickens at one time. Plus we had riding horses and workhorses."[49]

Even vacations consisted of work, C. L. recalled. "In the fall we had a 'corn picking vacation.' This was supposed to be fun, but we didn't think so at the time. My dad would pick two rows of corn in the time it took my little brother and me to pick one row. I was never involved in sports or anything. Back then, as soon as you got out of school for the day, you went to work on the farm. There's just no end to it. I wouldn't say we hated it—we didn't know any better."[50]

A Seed Is Planted

At 7, C. L. learned to drive a tractor, and by age 10 he was driving farm trucks and pickup trucks. Driving had a grand appeal over other farm labors and confirmed C. L.'s suspicion—the farm was not his calling.

"In the mid- to late 1950s, [I realized] that farming wasn't going to be very good for me," C. L. recollected. "I had more ambitions than to put in a lot of hours of work and make very little money."[51] The Nebraska drought had taken a toll on farming, which added to C. L.'s eagerness to leave the family business.

In 2003 C. L.'s parents are alive and well—his father 89 and his mother 87. "They were good parents, and they worked hard raising seven of us," C. L. said.

They grew up through the Depression, so they weren't risk takers. They were very happy to get their farms paid for and feed their family. That's where I disagreed with my dad because I would have been leveraging the farm to buy more. I got out on my own because he wasn't about to do anything risky. But that was good, and I can see why now. If I had been raised in that era, I would have probably been the same way. But I had nothing to lose. He did. I could go out with my car and start leveraging everything, and I could borrow and get into business and not look back, but I had a different outlook on life than what farmers did.[52]

Hence in 1956, 19-year-old C. L. Werner bid farewell to the family farm and headed to Omaha in pursuit of his role in life.

C. L. Werner began his trucking career in this 1956 Ford in the midst of a heavily regulated industry.

THE LONG HAUL BEGINS
1956–1966

It is a rough road that leads to the heights of greatness.

—from *Epistles*, by Roman philosopher Seneca

ARRIVING IN OMAHA VIRTUALLY penniless, C. L. Werner needed work. He had someone else to support—wife Gloria, whom he married in the fall of 1956. The couple rented a room from C. L.'s aunt and uncle, and C. L. took a hard-labor job in a steel mill. But punching a time clock was unnatural to C. L., and 40 hours in the steel mill felt like 90 hours on the farm. He began to recognize his longing for independence, a need to control his own destiny.[1]

After about a month, C. L. set his sights on moving out of breakout casting and into a job as a forklift operator. It turned out that 40 other men wanted the same post, and C. L. found himself at the bottom of a 12-year waiting list.[2]

"A month at the mill was about all I could handle," C. L. recalled. "I didn't like waiting for a whistle to blow to tell me I could eat my lunch. So I left."[3]

C. L. began thinking like an entrepreneur, and a new plan emerged. He had one tangible asset: a 1953 Mercury. Using his car as a down payment, he bought a 1956 Ford truck. "My parents were the only ones attending church in an 18-wheeler," daughter Gail Werner-Robertson would later remark.[4]

Being just 19, C. L. could haul only within Nebraska. The real money, however, was in hauling interstate, for which the driver had to be 21. Fortunately for C. L. Werner, a doctor's certificate was the standard document used as proof of age, and when C. L. had received his, the print on the document was smeared and illegible. The age listed looked as much like 21 as it did 19. He obtained his interstate license and was off and running.[5]

Regulation: An Obstacle and a Blessing

Small operations such as C. L.'s were usually hired on a per-trip basis. C. L. would haul grain to one location and then "trip lease" for a steel or lumber company, delivering the return load to a destination somewhere in the direction of home.

At the time, the Interstate Commerce Act regulations were the biggest obstacles for truckers. The act granted exclusive "authority" to certain truckers to haul products across state lines. Invariably, this authority flowed to established trucking companies. Small haulers stood no chance. "When you start with one truck, you have a million competitors," C. L. soon learned.[6]

It made no difference whether Werner's services were specifically requested by a customer. "The only

---

C. L. Werner at his desk in his first office, in Council Bluffs, Iowa way you could get authority was if the service was not already available," C. L. recalled. "You couldn't even mention rates at a hearing. The [Interstate Commerce Commission (ICC)] judges knew it was rigged, but nobody would say anything."[7]

But C. L. saw only opportunities. "Regulation was God's blessing," he said in retrospect. "That's what made us the company we are today. Regulation kept all the good freight from us. All we got was what the large carriers didn't want. So we had to have low costs. We had to pound every penny out of that."[8]

The crumbs left by the large carriers consisted mostly of unprofitable commodities exempt from ICC regulations (anything manufactured was nonexempt). "You had to be a commodity marketer, and that's what I was for quite a while," C. L. said. "I hauled rock and gravel in the winter, grain in the spring, and produce in the summer."[9]

C. L. ran the entire business from his 900-square-foot home for the first six years. He was salesman, driver, mechanic, and bookkeeper. The hours were endless. His eldest son, Gary, born in 1957, recalled his father's dedication.

Left: This 1966 Freightliner was one of only 12 trucks owned by Werner at the time. Today it is displayed in the Werner Museum.

Opposite: A replica of C. L. Werner's first truck, a 1956 Ford, left, and a 1958 GMC tractor, right, are among other antiques on display in the museum.

1956 — C. L. Werner arrives in Omaha, Nebraska, and takes a job in a steel mill. One month later he buys a truck to start his own business venture.

1957 — Son Gary Werner is born.

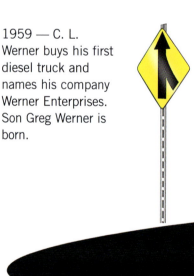

1959 — C. L. Werner buys his first diesel truck and names his company Werner Enterprises. Son Greg Werner is born.

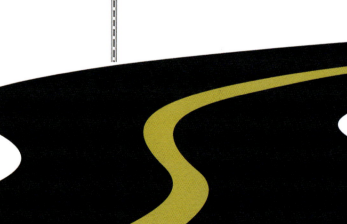

CHAPTER TWO: THE LONG HAUL BEGINS

"I remember when I was very young . . . he'd be working on the truck out in the street in front of our house. He didn't have a shop to work in then. If the weather wasn't good, there was this old viaduct he could pull the truck under and work on it and stay dry."[10]

Upgrading

In 1959 C. L. named his company Werner Enterprises and purchased his first diesel truck, an 860 GMC, which changed the stakes completely. He bought a second one later that year. "I didn't make any money with that Ford truck. I just made a living," C. L. said. "The diesels ran on less fuel, and it was cheaper. Back then diesel fuel was 20 cents a gallon. Gas was 35 cents. And I got two-and-a-half miles to a gallon with the Ford, and the diesels would get five."[11]

The new trucks formed the foundation of C. L.'s growth plan. As he paid off his trucks, he traded his first diesel in for two. When those two

1962 — C. L. hires his first driver, Ronnie Nelson. Daughter Gail Werner is born.

1964 — C. L. buys land in Council Bluffs, Iowa, and builds Werner Enterprises' first facility. Son Curt Werner is born.

were paid for, he traded them in for four, and so on. He would maintain this "one-for-two" practice well into the 1970s.

Building the Werner Family

Of course, more trucks meant more drivers. "That's when you start learning about people," C. L. said. "As long as I could have [a driver] running right along with me, we did really well. But then I'd turn him loose somewhere, and that's when things really started to happen."[12]

Some of C. L.'s early encounters with drivers were interesting, daughter Gail recalled.

Some of the drivers had ongoing problems controlling the cash they were given. They were given large sums of cash to cover all of their operating costs on the road: fuel, repairs, and miscellaneous costs. It was fairly common for the drivers to be robbed, so many of our drivers carried guns, including my dad. So when Dad moved from truck to desk, his revolver went with him because he had large quantities of cash in his desk. We had our own Wild West–Jesse James stories.[13]

Luckily, the average driver caused less dangerous problems. "They'd lay [low] somewhere for a day," C. L. recalled. "Or they'd haul an extra load and keep the money . . . all kinds of things. So you'd learn all that as you go along."[14]

With little use of credit cards in the late 1950s and early 1960s, business was transacted on a cash basis. When a driver left on a trip, he was supplied enough cash to complete the job or was wired additional money while on the road. However, there was no fail-safe way to track the money.

One of the most common scams involved tire tubes. It was easy for a rogue driver to get a phony receipt from a service station for a tire inner tube, expense it to the company, and split the money with the mechanic. But C. L. ended this scam by requiring, in addition to the regular receipt, a duplicate receipt tucked between the tire and the inner tube. Periodically, tires would be pulled back in Council Bluffs to verify the charges.

"Those tubes were 20 or 30 bucks," C. L. recalled. "That's like 100 bucks today—or pretty near 200. We even caught a few swiping some of the little receipt [pads] and making false receipts."[15]

But most drivers in the late 1950s and early 1960s were honest, hardworking employees dealing with poor, low-horsepower equipment. (Engines averaged between 160 and 220 horsepower.) Trucks of the day not only crept along but also broke down often, obliging drivers to have mechanical skills. Drivers traveled between 100,000 and 120,000 miles per year on mostly poor highways at a pay rate of between 6 and 8 cents per mile. In addition, very few trucks had sleeper cabs, and most of the drivers slept over

---

C. L. Werner remembers his company's earliest drivers with great affection. The late Russell Scott, left, and Gail Hammitt, right, are among them.

their steering wheels night after night while on the road; few truck stops offered shower and sleeping facilities.[16]

Eliminating Cash

In an effort to curb temptation, C. L. had drivers stop only at certain truck stops. This measure became possible when the company began running regular routes. The most notable route headed south into Texas and Louisiana. Another ran west through Wyoming into Idaho and Utah. As a result, a rapport with service providers along the way gradually grew. The stations were aware of how much repeat business C. L. was sending their way, and they appreciated his regular drivers: They were neat and clean and never caused trouble, unlike the stereotypical roughnecks that frequented the stations.

C. L. drew on the goodwill he had established. "I said, 'Now, I've been dealing with you guys for two, three years. . . . Is there any way you could set me up a charge, and I'll pay you the minute you send me the invoice at the end of the month? Or I'll even pay you in two weeks.'"[17]

To his surprise, every one of the vendors extended credit for 30 days. This was a major step for the company. By solving the problem of possible misappropriation of funds by drivers, C. L. had also freed up a great deal of operating capital.

Recognizing these benefits, he adopted a proactive policy when it came to paying his creditors. Even though his vendors offered terms of 30 days, C. L. cut a check the day the bill arrived and mailed it immediately, reinforcing his reputation for running a first-rate organization.

The regular stops provided a communications channel as well. If an emergency arose, a driver could be tracked down by calling the stops along the route. "You'd say, 'My driver will come in there, and he needs to call immediately.' That's the only communication you had with them."[18]

Hauling Nonexempt

C. L. avoided the problematic regulation issues and turned a profit by purchasing the goods he wanted to haul. Technically there was no carrier; he was simply a broker taking his goods to market. The revenue wasn't coming directly from trucking, but the truck was an integral part of the equation.

In 1963 C. L.'s third cousin, Wayne Childers, became his first major nonexempt commodity client. Childers was in the lumber business and worked for the William T. Joyce Company in Council Bluffs, Iowa. He recalled C. L.'s first visit.

I didn't really know [C. L.], even though we were shirttail relations. He came into my office one day looking for something to do. He wanted to know if there was anything he could haul. Back in those days, everything was done by railroad. The problem was that the railroads were unreliable—it would sometimes take 30 days to run a carload of lumber from Louisiana to Council Bluffs, where the main warehouse was located.[19]

Frustrated with the railroads, Childers struck an agreement with C. L. "We worked under a buy-sell arrangement," Childers recalled. "He would buy the lumber from my mill, haul the lumber up to me, and I would pay him. That's the only way we could do it legally."[20]

Childers saw the need for C. L. to expand his small fleet of trucks.

All he had was an old, beat-up truck, and of course that wouldn't go to Louisiana and back very many times without breaking down. So he had a conversation with the bank, and as a result, they came down to see me. A couple of gentlemen from the local bank in Council Bluffs wanted to make sure he really did have a customer, and I said, "Absolutely. If he can perform, he's going to have all of my lumber from the South." As a direct result of that, they lent him the money to buy three brand-new GMC tractors. Then he bought three grain trailers to go with them, and he would haul grain down to Arkansas to the chicken and turkey growers and then drop down to Louisiana and pick up my lumber and bring it back. It was a tremendous deal for him. He could make a trip or a round and a half a week pretty easily and make pretty good money.[21]

KNIGHTS OF THE ROAD

Truckers in the 21st century and truckers in the 1950s share many traits. Their right boot sole is worn thin. They see the world from six feet above the rest of us. They still follow that endless white line with a sense of freedom. But the modern trucker is also very different from the truckers who paved the way.

Equipment was certainly inferior. "The trucks were terrible compared to today," C. L. Werner said. "They were underpowered and broke down a lot. I remember my first trip in the mountains . . . going four miles per hour on the way up.

"You had to be halfway mechanical to drive trucks back then. A driver was expected to work on the truck he drove. It was almost like his own truck."

When Werner Enterprises started rolling in 1956, drivers were jacks of all trades. They understood the nuts and bolts of the trucking operation. "They had to think on their own," C. L. said. "Today, everything is handled for them by dispatchers and support people."

Wages have also changed. In the 1960s truckers worked for five cents a mile. "It was a factory worker's wage," C. L. said. "Today they make a lot more than factory wage."

In those days truckers were known as the knights of the road. "Truckers looked out for each other," C. L. said. "Today drivers know that everyone has cell phones, and they are less inclined to stop. Back then, they were the knights of the road. They helped everyone."[1]

Childers and C. L. Werner soon expanded their deal to include a manufacturing mill in Wyoming. "Clarence would haul soybean meal out to Salt Lake City, Utah, and then he'd drive up to Afton, Wyoming, and pick up a load of house studs and bring them back," Childers said. "That was the next part of the operation."[22]

Earning Respect

C. L.'s business tactics made an impression on many—even a teenage Jeff Doll, now a Werner director. Doll's father ran a family business, beer and wine distributor Accounts Plus. C. L. was a small carrier for the Dolls. "I've admired [C. L.] for a very long time," Doll said. "Even when he was a budding entrepreneur, you could see there was greatness in him. He had a presence about him. You just knew he was going places."[23]

In 1964 C. L. Werner hired his first accountant, Zeph Telpner, CPA. Werner Enterprises was still a

---

Jeff Doll was 16 when he met C. L. Werner. Today he is on the board of directors of Werner Enterprises.

very young company with nominal earnings, and Telpner's accounting firm was just six months old.

"My spouse and four kids were hungry, and [C. L.] must have known," Telpner recalled. When Telpner handed C. L. his first tax return, C. L. asked, "How much do I owe you?"

"No one else had ever paid me when I delivered the return, so I didn't have the bill with me," Telpner recalled. Telpner estimated the bill to be $100, and C. L. handed over $125. "That was a sacrifice for [C. L.]," Telpner said.[24]

During those early years, both men kept late hours, unable to pay others for what they could accomplish themselves. "Once at 4 A.M. I was disgusted with my long hours," Telpner said. "I phoned the only friend that I knew would still be working—Clarence. He was repairing a tractor."[25]

Conrad Heinson, founder of Allied Oil and Supply, was one of C. L.'s earliest vendors. "He's been a very loyal customer," Heinson said. "And I never had a contract. I always enjoyed Clarence's counsel, his friendship, and his business. In fact, he is my biggest account today."[26]

Heinson noticed C. L.'s foresight to hire the best employees early on. "His ability to hire and secure smart people is very professional," he said. "I think that is where he's excelled."[27]

Setting Up Shop

By 1965 Werner Enterprises had about a dozen trucks, all metallic blue, and nearly $550,000 in annual revenue. By that time, C. L. had stopped driving in order to oversee his growing company. It was time to move Werner Enterprises out of his home.

C. L. found an acre and a half of land in Council Bluffs, a small community just across the Missouri River from Omaha. He paid $25,000 for the property and built a little shop and office. C. L.'s second son, Greg, recalled, "We were running around making balls with clay from the footings. We didn't have Play-Doh®."[28]

Out of that same clay, C. L. began molding what would become his empire. By the late 1960s he had built and nurtured a solid business. But the trucking market was still cutthroat and heavily regulated. Survival in this tenuous environment helped forge C. L. Werner's company

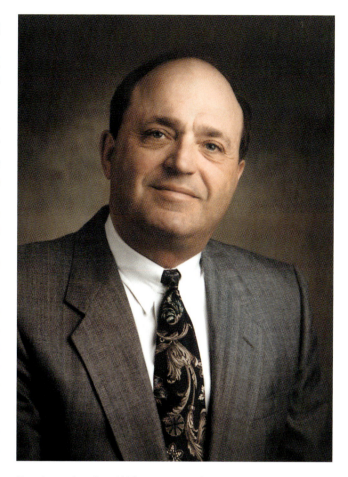

Board member Gerald Timmerman said Werner's ability to operate in crisis mode has bred success.

philosophy, said Gerald Timmerman, Werner Enterprises board member and longtime associate of C. L.

This company's philosophy is that you've got to stay on the leading edge of technology, keep your costs in line, [maintain a] high service level, and keep that work ethic in place. I believe this company, like all successful companies, has got to continue to operate in crisis mode. I know that's a philosophy here. It creates an opportunity for growth.[29]

Everything was in place at Werner Enterprises: technology, work ethic, and solid service. As for operating in "crisis mode," C. L. Werner's crises began with getting out of bed each morning.

"It seemed everybody had a truck," recalled Timmerman. "It was competitive, and the equipment wasn't as good as it is today. You really had to be enterprising to grow and make money. I think C. L. had that entrepreneurial and business spirit early on."[30]

Duane Acklie, chairman of Crete Carrier Corporation of Nebraska, also witnessed C. L.'s early struggles. "He always was a focused, dedicated person," Acklie recalled. "Trucking is a tough industry. It's not like others, where you have big opportunities to have a great percentage of profit. It's a penny business. As long as you recognize that, and as long as you believe that the future is great, it'll *be* great. And that was always Clarence's belief."[31]

The Werner Family Joins the Werner Business

By the late 1960s C. L. had another workforce waiting impatiently in the wings: his four children. Early employee Donna Johnson recalled the Werner children's early involvement.

It was absolutely a family business. The older boys, Gary and Greg, would come to the offices, and after they worked so many hours, they could work on their cars in the shop. And Gail used to come in in the evenings and clean. Those kids worked hard. They didn't slough off. They didn't have to be yelled at. It was really a happy family business.[32]

It's not surprising that C. L.'s children, Gary, Greg, Gail, and Curt, took an early interest in the business, said Gail Werner-Robertson. "Our parents both worked in the business, and that's all that was talked about at the dinner table. So you felt left out if you weren't involved in what was going on day to day."[33]

Gail, born in 1962, would later realize that not all households were devoted to nurturing a company. "I thought it was a normal childhood," she said. "I didn't know that other people didn't talk at their dinner tables about trucks, employees, taxes, and [Internal Revenue Service] and [Department of Transportation] auditors. Nor did they get phone calls in the middle of the night when there was an accident. We all dreaded hearing that phone ring at 2 A.M."[34]

The Werners even spent family vacations scoping out their father's competitors. "My Dad could find every possible shipping dock within a 20-mile radius of our vacation spot," Gail recalled. "If he didn't see a Werner truck there, the sales department at Werner would be getting a phone call."[35]

"Trucking is all I've ever known," said eldest son Gary Werner. "I remember riding in the truck with my Dad when I was very young, probably 3 or 4 years old. I always wanted to ride in the truck. He took me when he could—weekends or short trips."[36]

Gary's earliest duties were mowing and weeding the grass around the shop. As he got older, he began changing oil in trucks in the service bays and eventually changed tires and performed heavier maintenance. Just like his father, Gary had an affinity with equipment.[37]

Greg Werner, born in 1959, was not far behind. He developed a penchant for body work and restoration. "I used to actually [freehand] paint the decals and numbers on the trucks and the trailers," Greg said. "I was also very good at changing tires. I worked in the shop quite a bit and kind of bounced around different areas. I liked doing different things. I remember helping the guys rebuild Detroit engine [cylinder] heads."[38]

Gary and Greg enjoyed the work so much that C. L. started a small business for them: Gra-Gar. Curt and Gail would join as they grew older. Gra-Gar leased out equipment and at one time even had a warehouse. Years later, the small company would fuse with Werner Enterprises, and Greg would continue to use its small machine shop to manufacture parts and build and restore old cars and bikes.[39]

However, no one was forced to work—they begged to do it. "I always wanted to work at my Dad's shop," said Curt Werner, who was born in 1964. "I bugged and begged him for a chance. I was pretty relentless. I think I was about 12 years old when he said, 'OK, you can come up to the shop and we'll find a few things for you to do.'"[40]

Gail said the siblings argued over how young they could begin working. "We were involved from the time we could walk. We started very, very young."[41]

Curt recalled watching his father at work.

It was amazing growing up with him. It seemed like everywhere we went, even when we were a small trucking company, everybody knew my Dad. I was fascinated by how many people he knew. You have to be quite a charismatic person to network and know all these people. And they liked him. Even at a young age, I saw that.[42]

Greg said, "I was lucky that my older brother, Gary, had his license. We would drive to work together after school."[43]

Everyone began at the bottom, pulling weeds or mowing grass. As the children matured, so did their roles in the company. Gail moved into a receptionist position, and the boys gravitated to the shop.

Shop work was not glamorous; equipment and facilities were fairly crude. "We had old rock and mud parking lots, and the equipment was way different from what it is today," Greg recounted. "Brakes used to freeze up. . . . They'd freeze to the ground, and you'd have to jack them up and break them away from the ground in the wintertime."[44]

Curt was eager to get a uniform. "Eventually, I got it going into the shop. I worked on trucks like my brothers—wheel seals, tires changes, and

These were familiar faces at Werner Enterprises early on. From left are Greg, 6; Gail, 3; Curt, 1; and Gary, 8.

quick service, . . . not overly complicated stuff. We had some very good mechanics, and I got to help out. I learned a lot about equipment."[45]

C. L. Werner, right, and Freightliner representative Don Mercer seal the deal on the first major purchase of 10 tractors in 1971.

CHAPTER 3

BUILDING THE WERNER FAMILY
1967–1975

Their people stay with them a long time. You rarely see turnover at Werner Enterprises.

—Gale Wickersham, longtime business associate

DURING WERNER'S BUDDING years, C. L. hand-selected employees. He knew that in a company the size of his, each person would have a major impact. Consequently, his selection process was unusual.

Cecil Curry, for example, was never expected to work. At the age of 7 he was stricken with polio. By age 12, Curry had undergone three operations. He would wear a brace on his right leg for the rest of his life.

Despite his disability, Curry was independent, making him ideally suited to the Werner company culture. "There was nothing I couldn't do," Curry said emphatically. "Matter of fact, I can do things that some people with two legs can't do."[1]

"Cecil drove for me when I had just four trucks," C. L. said. "He's real strong up top, so he could pull himself up on those flatbeds and tarp them."[2]

Curry's career at Werner spanned 31 years and began in 1967, in the days when Werner hauled grain and lumber. Curry recalled the "drop trailers." These piano-hinged trailers were one of C. L. Werner's creations. They served as a provisional step between flatbeds and vans and moved the company closer to hauling regulated freight. The design allowed a flatbed trailer with collapsible, hinged sides to haul goods such as grain. "We were hauling air conditioners for Kimberly Clark using the drop trailers," Curry said. "You just drove in, dropped your side panels, clipped the side panels back on, and you were loaded."[3]

Years later, Curry would witness the beginning of Werner's transition to vans. "Clarence started getting trailers because they were lighter and had a stronger floor in them," Curry remembered. "You could haul more of a load."[4]

While Cecil Curry was tending to Werner's growth on the outside, his wife, Sharon Curry, was busy building the office support needed for the emerging company.

Sharon came to Werner through roundabout circumstances. As a meter maid for the Council Bluffs, Iowa, Police Department in 1971, Sharon wrote C. L. a parking ticket. "I knew it was his car," she said, "but I had to give him a ticket anyway. Otherwise I'd get turned in."[5]

C. L. struck up a conversation with her and before long asked if she would consider working for him. Handing him his ticket, she told him she would think about it. Within a few days, Sharon gave two weeks' notice at the police department.[6]

The Freightliner truck was an early workhorse for Werner Enterprises.

Sharon set up her first office in the tire shop and took on the bookkeeping and permitting.

I had to keep track of all those drivers' hours, all their accidents, the fuel reports, and the licensing of the trucks. Each one had to be licensed in every state. I was responsible for getting all the permits onto the trucks, and if a truck came in at 3 o'clock in the morning, they'd have a note in their drivers' room to call me at home.[7]

At 3 or 4 A.M., Sharon would head to the terminal to place permits in drivers' books and make sure things were in order. "You didn't leave them out on the board," she explained, "because other drivers could come in and take the wrong permit."[8]

Sharon and Cecil Curry knew from the beginning that they were part of history in the making, and Cecil began documenting the Werner experi-

Driver Cecil "Mark" Curry, hired in 1967, stands with his first flatbed trailer in 1971. Despite a physical disability, Curry's career at Werner Enterprises spanned 31 years.

1971 — C. L. Werner hires his first office employee, Sharon Curry.

1971 — C. L. makes his first big truck purchase: 10 new Freightliner trucks.

1971 — Donna Johnson is hired to obtain authority for Werner Enterprises.

1972 — Jim Larsen is hired to oversee the new van division.

CHAPTER THREE: BUILDING THE WERNER FAMILY

ence with photographs. He amassed hundreds of pictures throughout his career, and many of them are displayed in the Werner Museum at the company's headquarters.

Going after Authority

Gradually, C. L. added to his team. But he found there were few qualified people in the area to choose from, and persuading skilled people to come aboard a start-up company was no easy feat. Not only did he have to convince them that he provided a better place to work, C. L. also had to convince them that his growing trucking company was going places—that Werner was going to be around, not just next year, but for the next 20 years.

C. L. needed someone who knew how to get the proper authority for securing regulated freight. Brokering nonregulated freight and commodities was proving to be an enormous amount of work for an uncertain payoff. Regulated business was where the money was. C. L. hired Donna Johnson, who had worked for a transportation attorney for seven years.

"When I started in 1971, the company operated only flatbed trailers," Johnson said.

1975 — Werner Enterprises secures the Maytag account, its first *Fortune* 500 customer.

"They'd go from Iowa and Nebraska up to the Northwest with grain, and they'd come back with lumber. They never went past the Mississippi River."[9]

C. L.'s drop trailers were ideal for business then. "They'd put the sides up, line it, and haul grain up," Johnson explained. "And then they'd put them down and haul lumber, or sometimes Christmas trees, back."[10]

Getting into Vans

Shortly after Johnson was hired, she applied for temporary authority to haul for Skinner Macaroni. A man named Robert Crawford had the authority, but he was ill and needed help. "Temporary authority wasn't that hard to obtain," Johnson said.[11]

But the account required vans for hauling. C. L. recalled his first big purchase.

In 1971 we bought 10 trucks from a Freightliner dealer in Omaha, Floyd Huff. He was always dressed to a T and always wore a hat. The reason I bought from him was because he believed in me, and he'd get my trucks financed for me. I had a good, reliable source of service right there in town. I'd have to say that it was mostly Mr. Huff who got me going. He was a very dominating person, but very fair, and he could figure a trucker out real quick—whether he had a chance of making it. If he did, [Mr. Huff] would be doing business with him.

That same year we also bought 10 flatbed trailers from Miles Gagnon at Salt Lake City Utility Trailer Company. That was the beginning of a long business relationship and a lifelong friendship with the Gagnon family.

We also bought eight Kenworth trucks from Rod French at Mid-Iowa Kenworth in Des Moines.[12]

A year later, Werner received full authority to buy Crawford's rights to the Skinner Macaroni account for $25,000. Johnson had played a major role in obtaining the company's first major authority. But her knowledge of authority rights and equipment were two different things. "I actually had to ask Clarence what the difference was between a flatbed and a van," Johnson said.[13]

Much to her surprise, C. L. didn't chastise her. "He laughed a little," she said. "Then he took me out back and showed me."[14]

Johnson continued to obtain more authority for Werner Enterprises and even managed to beat her former boss, the attorney, in several cases.

Johnson reminisced, "We slowly built up our clientele. . . . You do almost everything when you're that small and there are only five people in the office. When I started work, I had a card table—no desk or anything. We kept records in books, about

Werner's first big purchase of 10 trucks enabled the company to take on accounts such as Maytag and Griffin Pipe Products.

C. L. AND THE EXTRA MILE

IN THE EARLY DAYS AT WERNER, JIM Larsen (below) was C. L.'s right-hand man. "Without him, I probably wouldn't be here today," C. L. said. "I hired him in 1972 at $400 a week. That was unheard of. I wasn't drawing that much out of this company, but he was worth it."

But in the midst of this dynamic relationship, tragedy struck. Larsen was diagnosed with a brain aneurysm. Doctors deemed it inoperable and gave him less than a month to live. However, the doctors had never seen the Werner/Larsen team in the face of adversity.

"[Doctors] wouldn't do anything for him here," C. L. said. "We found out about this doctor from Scotland or Ireland who came to Chicago every month and operated on people with aneurysms. Jim was ready to die. He was allergic to all the medicine they gave him, and he had this terrible humming and banging in his head. Couldn't even work."

C. L. saw only one way to save his friend and confidant's life and took the initiative. "I flew Jim and his wife and daughter to Chicago. The doctor only gave him a 50-50 chance," C. L. said. "They operated for eight hours. They had to quit tying the veins off because [the doctor] said Jim would die if he stayed in there any longer, he was losing so much blood."

That was more than 25 years ago, and Jim Larsen has since retired. But not before returning to work for many years and finishing his career at Werner. "[The doctor] saved him," C. L. said, downplaying his own role in the circumstances. "He came back and worked for years. I saw Jim not too long ago, and he still looks pretty good. Lost his hair," he joked, "but he looks pretty good."[1]

20 inches by 12. Each truck was numbered, and the mileage was recorded by hand."[15]

In C. L.'s words, "We ran the company back then just like we run it today. Very, very conservatively."[16]

Handling the New Load

While Johnson was busy securing transportation authority for the company, C. L. needed someone dedicated to the day-to-day running of the new van division. C. L. recruited Jim Larsen in 1972.

"I was running a small truckline for a guy over in Omaha, and Clarence was in [Council Bluffs, Iowa]," Larsen recalled. "My boss wanted to sell that truckline and move to Texas. In the meantime, Clarence had been coming over there and sitting in the office a lot and I guess just listening to me on the phone. He knew I wasn't going to stay where I was, so he made me a pretty nice offer."[17]

C. L. and Larsen quickly developed a rapport. "[Larsen] was a high-caliber guy who knew trucking," C. L. recalled. "He was the greatest guy in the world to handle drivers and customers. I had to go out and sell, and I knew he could handle the whole thing. He was sharp, and he knew how to get along on the telephone. He wouldn't operate without two phones on his desk, and he would be on them at the same time."[18]

Larsen did everything for Werner Enterprises from hiring to customer service. Until then, the vans hadn't been fully utilized; that changed quickly. "There was another fellow handling flatbeds," Larsen said. "I took over the vans, which were all sitting when I took them. I don't think there was one on the road the day I started. Most of them were sitting there loaded, but drivers were a problem. We got them all emptied out rather rapidly because I had a couple of accounts I took with me."[19]

About this time, Werner had secured the authority for the Skinner Macaroni account.

Larsen had dealt with Skinner in the past and was aware of how demanding the company could be. "[The Skinner account] called me up and told me I was crazy for changing companies, and I said, 'Well, I don't think so.' He said, 'Well, we'll just see how good they are. I want three trailers in here tomorrow at six o'clock [in the morning].'"[20]

Larsen didn't have three available trailers. Everything on the lot was loaded. He knew, however, that passing this test was essential to landing what could become a staple account for Werner.[21]

C. L. had Larsen round up three empty trailers in Round Lake, Minnesota, for the job. "From that time on, [Skinner was] a major account," Larsen said.[22] The new account helped Werner Enterprises reach revenues of $1.45 million in 1972.

Early Authority

C. L. continued to secure at least partial authority for several shippers. Two key accounts were Griffin Pipe Products and Maytag.

Griffin Pipe Products, located in Council Bluffs, Iowa, is a manufacturing plant for cast iron pipe and water mains. The site of Werner's first terminal and office was just a short distance away. John Keenan, former director of purchasing and traffic for Griffin Pipe, recalled, "Clarence had approximately 10 power units and maybe 20 flatbed trailers. So it was a nice start-up, and he was a great help to us."[23]

At the time, much of Werner's business was hauling lumber. Because one of the first things that goes into a new subdivision is the water and sewer system, and because the lumber business serves new housing construction, the alliance between Griffin and Werner was ideal.

Complementary relationships aside, Keenan had his own reasons for selecting Werner for his business. "Clarence was a man of integrity," Keenan said. "If he said he would do something for you, a handshake was good enough. You didn't need a contract. Secondly, Clarence knew trucks mechanically, and he knew how to buy the most efficient truck to keep costs down. Thirdly, he knew how to treat his employees [and] be fair with them, and they all worked hard as a team."[24]

The relationship between Griffin Pipe and Werner flourished, and Keenan witnessed Werner's growth firsthand. He observed how Werner landed the Maytag account. "Clarence, as the story goes, was sitting at his breakfast table with the television on," Keenan said.

I believe the program was "Good Morning America." The story was about a Maytag industrial plant in Newton, Iowa, which manufactures washing machines and things. They were in very big trouble because the railroad that serviced that plant, Rock Island Railroad, was filing Chapter 11 bankruptcy. That railroad [had] hauled many, many piggyback truckloads of washing machines from Newton, Iowa, to the far West every day. Clarence jumped in the car and drove to Newton.

He met with the traffic manager and told him that he had a good trucking company with a lot of high-cube vans to haul washing machines with. I understand that immediately a relationship was struck with Maytag. In the first year, I think Clarence did over $1 million in revenue with Maytag.[25]

The relationship with Maytag began in 1975 and marked a major breakthrough for C. L. and his company. In fact, Maytag was Werner's first *Fortune* 500 account. Lee Hays, Maytag's traffic manager, recalled his first meeting with C. L. "C. L. was dressed in blue jeans, cowboy boots, and a huge belt buckle. He also had an Afro hairdo. I thought, 'Who is this guy?' We had an immediate chemistry."[26]

The only obstacle was that Werner didn't have authority to serve Newton, Iowa, or the cities where Maytag needed to ship. "I agreed I would support his application before the Interstate Commerce Commission for authority to handle our products," Hays said.[27]

Though Maytag utilized a number of motor carriers, the Rock Island line failure created a significant void in Maytag's shipping ability. Consequently, the application for authority was promptly approved. "I was anxious as to how much equipment C. L. really had, how many trailers we could count on for loading, because at that time we were probably loading up to 100 trailers a day. Clarence told me that he had 50 trailers. The thing that he neglected to tell me was that most of them were flatbed equipment. We needed the closed vans."²⁸

But C. L. was well ahead of the game. Anticipating receiving authority, he had ordered several vans. As Maytag called on Werner more and more, C. L. made sure to have equipment and personnel at the ready. "Werner did an outstanding job with our product," Hays said, "and word got around to our customers that Maytag was using a new truckline called Werner Enterprises that was doing a good job for us. We began getting more and more requests from our customers to use Werner."²⁹

The alliance between the two companies continued, and Werner became Maytag's primary distance carrier. The relationship continues to this day, as does the friendship forged by the two men.

I retired from Maytag more than eight years ago, but Maytag is still using Werner to a great extent. Clarence Werner and I got to be very good friends. I think a lot of him, and I think that he thinks a lot of me—more than a source of business and revenue.

*Clarence provided us with a great deal of equipment to ship our product, which we direly needed, and we gave him the business that helped him grow and buy more equipment. He was a joy to know, and I respect him mightily. From that old Afro hairdo, cowboy booted, belt buckled guy . . . he has certainly become a success.*³⁰

Building the Team

Werner Enterprises was a family to many. Wilbur Smith started in the shop in 1975, where the Werner boys pitched in. "They would come out and help me after school," Smith recalled. "They helped change oil in the trucks, change tires, put brakes on, and wash trucks."³¹

J. D. Farris was hired as a driver in 1974. "It was pretty well laid back," Farris said.

Mr. Werner, he was out with the troops every day. I mean he didn't keep to his office looking out the window. He came out and dealt with the

Mechanic Wilbur Smith, left, and driver J. D. Farris, right, were early members of the Werner Enterprises team.

*men and talked to you. He was a hands-on guy. Still is. He's not afraid to get his hands dirty, and he is a real compassionate man for his employees. If they needed financial help, he was there to help them. He was just one of the boys.*³²

New employees streamed in as the company grew. With C. L.'s sales acumen, Larsen's organization and communication abilities, and Johnson's persistence in seeking hauling authority, the van division grew steadily. Eventually growing pains set in, and the van division became too big for even Jim Larsen to handle. Always thinking ahead, he had someone waiting in the wings.

Larsen hired Buddy Payton, a driver from Macon, Georgia, in 1974. Payton was looking to move into an office job.

C. L. described Payton as "an old Southern boy." His father was a preacher in Georgia, and Payton was the last of a breed of drivers who wore ties. It didn't take long for him to secure work with Werner, first as a driver and then as a dispatcher.³³

As a driver, Payton was a seasoned professional and soon proved his dedication to the Werner team. These were the days when drivers had to be creative in the methods they used to make the barely profitable work pay. Grain haulers, for example, were notorious for hauling more than the legal weight limit, or running "heavy," during grain season.

"Everybody [else] was hauling heavy loads," Payton said. "We almost always ran legal."³⁴

The 15,000-square-foot shop at the new Werner Enterprises headquarters in Omaha provided space for up to 250 trucks.

CHAPTER 4

FULL SPEED AHEAD
1976–1979

I think you can credit our success not only to working hard but to thinking smart. To solve a problem, you don't just throw money at it. You fix it.

—C. L. Werner, 2002

THE DECADE THAT began with violence at Kent State and Jackson State Universities in protest of the Vietnam War ended with the Iranian hostage crisis. Against that uncertain backdrop, C. L. Werner was building a business that would grow beyond his wildest dreams.

C. L.'s remarkable business sense had kept the company growing even while the economy, checked by the 1973–74 embargo on Middle East oil imports, slogged through spiraling inflation, high unemployment, and stagnant product demand. Despite these grim conditions, no one was laid off at Werner Enterprises; in fact, as the rest of the country fell into a recession marked by gas shortages and corporate cutbacks, Werner continued to expand.

Onward and Upward

Expansion meant that C. L. Werner needed more square footage to accommodate his growing business. "We were outgrowing our landlocked, five-acre facility in Council Bluffs," C. L. recalled. "Fifty percent of my people lived in Omaha, Nebraska, and I could find more drivers in a bigger city."[1]

Dispatcher Jim Larsen lived in Louisville, Nebraska, about 10 miles south of Omaha and a 40-minute commute to the Council Bluffs office. "I was driving from Louisville to the Bluffs every morning about 5:30 or 6:00, and I was up there some nights until 7:30 or 8:00," Larsen recalled.

In those days, all we had for getting money to drivers was Western Union. I was the only one who could wire money, other than C. L. On weekends I'd have to run out two, three, four times to wire money. So I started more or less jokingly telling C. L. that he had to get a terminal closer to Louisville. I'd say, "I can't spend my entire life driving back and forth wiring money." We joked about it for some time. One day he went to lunch and came back, and he was grinning. He walked up to me and said, "Well, Larsen, you got your way. I just bought land over on [Interstate] 80 and Highway 50."[2]

Larsen had indeed gotten his wish—a 15-minute commute. But as kind as C. L. was, he hadn't made such a vital decision based on his dispatcher's wishes. The state of Iowa made the decision for him. In 1973, Iowa repealed its inter-

---

This sign was displayed with pride in Werner Enterprises' new entryway. The company moved its headquarters in 1976.

state carrier sales tax exemption, which meant trucking companies had to pay sales tax on equipment and parts.³ This added expense was justification enough for a move across the Missouri River into Nebraska, where these items were still tax exempt.⁴

At the time, Werner's routes ran in nearly 40 states. "Everywhere but the northeast coast," C. L. said.⁵ Building a facility at the junction of Interstate 80 and Highway 50 was a strategic move. Being situated on the edge of Omaha allowed the company access to all the provisions of the city without the in-town traffic. The new facility, C. L. said, "was right on the route my trucks use."⁶

Werner Enterprises broke ground for its Omaha facility in May 1976. "We were making pretty good money and growing pretty fast," C. L. said. "We built the facility without a loan."⁷

By then, Werner's gross sales had jumped from $3.9 million in 1975 to $6.1 million in 1976, and the company had 100 trucks on the road. The $450,000 facility would more than double the company's capacity with 30,000 square feet of office and shop space that could potentially accommodate 250 trucks.⁸ Laughlin Construction Company served as the general contractor.⁹

The new terminal housed offices, a large area for clerical and secretarial functions, a computer room, a lunchroom, and a conference room overlooking the interstate.¹⁰ C. L.'s office was finished with walnut paneling and decorated with paintings by actor Henry Fonda, bronze sculpture pieces, and a collection of Winchester rifles.¹¹

The 15,000-square-foot shop area contained a paint shop, two safety lanes, two service bays, a wash bay, seven maintenance bays, locker rooms, a parts room, and a storage area.¹²

C. L.'s daughter, Gail Werner-Robertson, had fond memories of the Omaha terminal, where she started working part-time at age 14.

I was very excited when we opened this facility here. I carpooled with my Dad that first summer, and I was a receptionist. It has been a huge advantage for me that I had the opportunity to grow up in a family where I was given tremendous responsibility at a very young age. I learned how to type there. I filed, typed reports, learned payroll.... By the time I was 18, I was running the accounts payable department.¹³

1976 — Werner breaks ground on its Omaha, Nebraska, headquarters.

1977 — Computers begin to play a role in Werner offices.

CHAPTER FOUR: FULL SPEED AHEAD 47

C. L. Werner, left, breaks ground in May 1976 for the Omaha, Nebraska, terminal with George Goos, of Lamp Ryerson Engineers, center, and Jerry Laughlin, of Laughlin Construction.

1978 — Werner buys its first aircraft, a Cessna 414.

1979 — C. L. Werner obtains a loan and expands his truck fleet.

The new terminal's safety lane provided multipoint inspections of every truck entering the terminal.

Getting Technical

With the new Omaha terminal complete, it was time to modernize the guts of the company. Expansion meant more paperwork, which had to be tracked. In 1977, Werner Enterprises purchased its first computer.[14]

"The cost of early computers was terrible, but we entered the computer age on the leading edge of technology because I knew that was the way to go," C. L. said. "Not that I'm very technical; I hardly do anything with my computer. But I had enough sense to know technology was the coming thing. When we first started looking at computers, I'd say, 'Ooh, that's a lot of money.' But it was the same as my equipment: I can't use yesterday's equipment and theories and be in business tomorrow. So I bit the bullet and went right into it."[15]

The jump into the information age was not the only transition the company made in the late 1970s. New departments were developing companywide, and C. L. needed several key personnel in a hurry. He didn't have to look far to find leaders. The close-knit group that had gotten the company that far was ready to spread out and step up.

Accounting was one of the first departments to delve into the burgeoning computer world. Werner Enterprises was a multi-million-dollar company, but its books were still kept by hand. Randy Dickerson, now chief accountant at Werner, became controller in 1978 and was accounting's one-man show for nearly six years. His predecessor had purchased a small computer and attempted to set up a system. It was Dickerson, however, who finally put the machine into play.

"It was kind of funny," Dickerson recalled. "When I started, there was a computer sitting there, and nobody even knew how it worked. There were no written instructions for it, and they hadn't closed the books for three months."[16]

Dickerson soon had the computer up and running. "I just took what they had and back-tracked my way into it," he said. "That's what I feel I'm good at. I take systems and create

> # REGULATIONS AND THE LEISURE SUIT
>
> SOME THINGS DO NOT WITHSTAND the test of time. What once seemed like a good idea can, in hindsight, appear more ridiculous with the passing of each day. For Greg Werner, two such items rightly went by the wayside in the late 1970s: regulation and the leisure suit.
>
> During the days of regulation, a young Greg had the opportunity to accompany his father to an authority hearing. "Dad took me along. I was excited," Greg said. "I remember I had on a blue leisure suit."
>
> "We went through the whole [regulation-authority] process," Greg continued. "We couldn't use cost savings as an issue. It had to be service-related issues or service failures. When I look back, all it served to do was to restrict commerce, to restrict competition. Any established old trucking company was pretty safe. Any new carrier with better service couldn't get into business. It was sewn up."
>
> Since that day, Greg draws an analogy between the daftness of regulation and the absurdity of the leisure suit. "I went through that whole process and had that blue leisure suit on. Now when I see any movie and I see [a leisure suit], I think, 'That's about how ridiculous the regulations were.'"[1]

new systems." Dickerson had single-handedly moved the accounting department into the world of automation.[17]

The approach of embracing rather than fighting change was permeating the company, as C. L. had long practiced. Dickerson explained, "I think what I've done over the years has really reflected what the company has done in general. We've changed our major computer system three or four times as we have grown. Change is probably the biggest word. We are not afraid of change. The way I do something today is totally different from the way I did it yesterday and the day before because that is just the way we operate. If we find a better way to do something, we're not afraid to do it."[18]

Catching On

The business office employed some 15 people, each clamoring for a computer. One of the voices rising above the crowd was that of longtime employee Donna Johnson. The new technology was ideally suited to her position as she worked to secure authority. But it wasn't as simple as Johnson had expected.

"I argued for a PC," Johnson said. "Well, they got me a PC all right. They came in and put a PC and all the paraphernalia on my desk. I didn't even know how to turn it on. 'Boot it up,' they said. I told them, 'I don't have boots on. How do you boot it up? Kick it?'"[19]

Soon after, employees at Werner Enterprises, Johnson among them, received a crash course in PCs.

On a grander scale, steps were being taken to install a companywide mainframe system. The understaffed dispatching department was the first area of concern. Dispatchers Jim Larsen, Buddy Payton, and Irv Chessareck were buried in work. And while computerization promised relief, it would not happen without the pains of change. Although their task seemed Herculean at times, they welcomed the challenge. The first step was research.

"Gary [Werner], Irv [Chessareck], Randy Ratekin, and I went up to National [Trucking]," Buddy Payton recalled. "They were a reefer [refrigerated truck] outfit, but they had a dispatch card system. Gary and the others went up to South Dakota and visited a company up there, too."[20]

The team decided on the Quantel 1 system, a very simple punch card system. Crude by 21st-century standards, it primarily addressed dispatching concerns. "Before we got the [Quantel 1 system], we did everything on spiral notebook and by memory," Payton said.[21]

Installing the system was no easy task, and at times the team members felt they were in over their heads. "Irv and I were busting our rear ends," Payton said. "We were working from six in the morning until midnight. Every night, we had to do everything—input the loads, get the mileage."[22]

Something had to give. "One day, Irv and I got up, and I said, 'Man, we've got to get some help around here.' So we walked into Gary Werner's office, and Gary said, 'What can I do for you?' And Irv said, 'WE QUIT!' I said, 'No we don't. Man, don't say *that!*' Gary asked what the matter was, and I said, 'Well, we're working pretty hard.'"

Gary offered the two men a $100-per-week raise if they could get the new program off the ground. Payton recalled, "I got out of my seat and said, 'I'm going back to work!'"[23]

The Quantel 1 system was eventually mastered by the dispatchers.

The usual trials and tribulations accompanied debugging and getting used to the new computers companywide, but when the dust settled, the team effort had paid off. "We came in on the weekends to iron out some of the bugs, but it really worked quite well," Johnson said.[24]

The Quantel 1 system was not the answer to all of Werner's information systems concerns, but it established some precedents. This first endeavor made clear the advantages of developing systems internally. "Almost all the systems have been created by people here at Werner," Johnson said. "So if there was something you were needing in [the system] that wasn't built into it yet, you could get it installed. That really helped a lot."[25]

It also made clear the ability of Werner employees to take on a project in an area completely unrelated to their backgrounds. "A lot of us didn't even know how to type. So C. L. sent about 16 of us to Metro Tech [a local community college] to take a typing course," said Payton.[26]

Keeping a Finger on the Pulse

C. L. Werner never allowed himself to forget the backbone of the company: the driver and the road. Twenty years after forming his company, he still made a point of climbing into a truck from time to time and taking a load out on the road. Many times these journeys were born out of necessity. "If I had a load sitting there, and the driver got sick or didn't show up, I'd take the truck myself and make the trip," he said.[27]

C. L. concerned himself with more than productivity, however. He wanted to know that his drivers were safe and content in their jobs. His daughter, Gail Werner-Robertson, recalled meeting some of the drivers while on these road trips with her father.

Almost every summer he would take a truck and just go on the road, just to take a load somewhere and kind of see what the drivers were experiencing. He wanted to see how the truck stops looked. He wanted to see how the shippers were treating our drivers. How were the trucks performing? Was the safety maintained? How was the maintenance? He would be in his cowboy boots and jeans, and off he'd go. He'd pull into a truck stop, and as the company was growing, there were almost always other Werner trucks at the stops. So we'd get out and go to visit some of the other Werner drivers, and they'd start talking about the company to him, having no idea who he was. So they're telling him all the good, the bad, and the ugly about the company. They would even tell him how they could soup the trucks up to make them go faster.[28]

C. L. knew his trucks. His grandfather had been a blacksmith and taught C. L. to weld. "He taught me how to do mechanics," he said. "My father was not a mechanic at all, so I wanted to learn all that. It really helped me when I got my first trucks. I didn't have to take them in to get brakes or wheels put on."[29]

When trucks were in accidents, even when they were completely totaled, C. L. and his team rebuilt them. "I'd work all night on them if I had to," C. L. recalled. "I had one mechanic back when I had 10 trucks. We did all our own body work. So I'm a pretty good body man. One of the first trailers I used to haul my trucks on I built myself at night in my shop. It's still out here, a lowboy trailer.

"Now we have people who are experts," C. L. said. "It changes as you get the size we are, but when you're small, it's so important to know every aspect of that business. You hire that driver. You know what he's going through and how fast he can get somewhere because you were out there, and you did it."[30]

Right and inset: Werner takes pride in its fleet, providing regular maintenance checks. Good equipment attracts good drivers, says Greg Werner.

Below: The 15,000-square-foot shop area in 1977 contained a paint shop, two safety lanes, two service bays, a wash bay, seven maintenance bays, locker rooms, a parts room, and storage.

A Boss and a Friend

IN 1977 DON BACON WAS DISCHARGED from the U.S. Air Force and began looking for work. His uncle worked at Werner Enterprises and steered Bacon toward a job in the company's service bay. He worked in the bay for about a year, then spent the next seven years in the office before becoming shop foreman.

One of the major undertakings at the time of Bacon's arrival was the building of the trailer shop at the new Omaha facility. The company didn't have a large enough fleet of trailers to fill it yet, but C. L. Werner had his eye on the future. In the meantime, the facility was put to use in other ways. Regulation still had a stranglehold on motor carriers, and Werner continued to deal regularly in commodities. Thus the trailer shop became a grain hopper.

"The first year we built the trailer shop, we filled it with corn," Bacon said. "They didn't have storage for corn, so they hauled it in from the farm, and they filled that building full of corn."

Bacon and C. L. spent many hours together while the shop was being built. Bacon recalled one of their early adventures. "C. L. had bought some 10,000- to 12,000-gallon fuel tanks. It was winter, and we were going to pick them up and haul them to C. L.'s farm. We left Omaha early in the morning in the dark in a cabover [truck] and the trailer that we used to haul the wrecked trucks on. My pickup truck was on that trailer. As we drove down the road, we realized the truck had no heat. I was driving and C. L. sat over on the other side. . . . I can still picture him wearing one of those leather caps with earmuffs that snapped up over the top. He was using a credit card to scrape the frost off the inside of the window so I could see. I told him, 'You know, C. L., this is a hell of a deal. Of all the trucks we have, we had to pick the one with no heat.'"

On the return trip, C. L. drove Bacon's heated pickup truck. "So we got the tanks and went back to the farm," Bacon laughed, "and I always thought it was kind of funny. Here I was driving that truck, and he was in my pickup with the heat."

Bacon poked fun at C. L.'s "survival" instincts, but he simultaneously extolled the man who always put his employees first.

"C. L. had a Ford truck. . . . I believe it was brand new at the time, and he was going to sell it," Bacon recalled. "I said, 'I'd like to buy that from you.' So I went to I don't know how many banks in Omaha, and no one would give me a loan. Not a soul. I went back to him and said, 'I'm sorry, C. L., I can't find anyone to loan me the money.' He said, 'Here, go to this bank and see so-and-so.' So I drove to the bank and asked for this guy and walked in, and he said, 'Here, sign your name right here.' I said, 'What?' and he said again, 'Just sign your name right here.' I suppose C. L. had called the bank."

Over the years Bacon came to play a role in a clever, light-hearted management tactic devised by C. L. to let his crew, particularly the dispatchers, know that he was aware of even their slightest corner cutting.

"When I was shop foreman, C. L. used to call me every two or three months, and he'd say, 'Don, I need a ride home,'" Bacon said. "This was usually about 6:30, . . . so I'd go over and pick him up, and he'd say, 'Let's go have a drink.' There was a bar just down the street from the office. We'd go in, and what do you know. The dispatchers, who were supposed to work late, every now and then [would] sneak out and go down and have a drink. So here comes the dispatcher, and he steps in the door and he'd stop. . . . He didn't leave because he was already caught. So he'd come in and sit down and have a drink. I don't know if C. L. ever said anything to the people or not; he just wanted to know what was going on."[1]

Werner Aviation

Having worn all the company hats, C. L. was no stranger to sales and marketing. When Werner Enterprises made the jump to its new facility, C. L. leaped to the next level of marketing. "He used to say, 'When I earn my first million, Donna, I'm going to buy airplanes,'" Donna Johnson recalled. "'Oh, yeah, right,' I laughed."[31]

But shortly after the company moved to Omaha, Werner Enterprises bought its first airplane, which quickly paid for itself as a sales tool. "Gary [Werner] and I did all the marketing," C. L. said. "I was in that plane all the time."[32]

"C. L. has a gift for being a tremendously good salesman," Greg Werner said. "He and Gary did a ton of sales in the early years. We didn't have a massive sales force when we were smaller, so they spent a tremendous amount of time doing the customer entertaining. Building that book of business is a lot of hard work, and they spent a ton of time doing that."[33]

Gary Werner had started working full-time for the company in 1977 and recalled, "It's amazing how much more productive C. L. and I were after getting the airplane. Some of our customers were located in small towns with limited or no commercial air service. We could now make three or four times as many sales calls in the same amount of time. The airplane allowed us to grow at a much faster rate than we could have otherwise."[34]

Werner's first aircraft was a Cessna 414, but before long the company upgraded to an E90 King Air, then a Super 200 King Air. The planes allowed C. L. and Gary to span the continent in pursuit of business. But upon arrival, they still had to sell the account. Already considered brilliant by his associates, C. L. turned these sales calls into another forum in which to shine.

Many believed C. L. was born with a photographic memory. More than likely, he developed it through his diligent pursuit of his business goals and dreams. "He spent a lot of time educating himself," Jim Larsen said. "When we used to travel, we'd get in a hotel, and the first thing he'd do is go out and get a hold of that *Wall Street Journal*. He'd spend hours in the morning reading it over before we'd have to go out and make calls."[35]

"It was always business, and, yes, he crossed it with pleasure," Gail added. "But he taught us at a very early age that you can mix both and that work is a never-ending thought process. You never rest on your laurels if you want to make your business and yourself better. It's never good enough. You're continuing to always search. What is the competition doing? What are we doing in connection to that? And how is the rest of the world changing? He had an ever questioning ability to analyze his business and how he was approaching it."[36]

The results of this ongoing self-education and development were obvious. C. L. was able to combine his mental gifts with his down-to-earth, humanistic ways to provide a no-nonsense, yet personable, approach. Even his youngest children accompanied him (typically individually) on sales calls in the plane, and each came away with the same experience, Gail said.

I think the thing that amazed me the most, we would be in a shipper's office, and C. L. would have nothing with him—not a calculator, not anything. He may have a pen and a truck model to give the individual, and that would be it.

On the way to the sales call, he would have already analyzed the routes we were doing with that shipper, he knew to the penny what we were making, and he'd sit in that meeting with nothing and calculate hundredweight rates. He'd convert mileage rates to hundredweight rates, and he'd strike a deal right then and there. And he was never afraid to tell them, "I've got to have two more cents," and the shipper [would have] his calculator out and would say, "Oh, that will be around $800 for the length," and C. L. would say, "Yeah, $804.02."[37]

Foretastes of Deregulation

By 1978, the new Omaha facility was completed, and its computer infrastructure was coming along well. Werner Enterprises was prepared for whatever came down the pike.

Revenues grew from $7.6 million in 1977 to $13.1 million in 1979. "We had enough authority that we were making pretty good money," C. L. recalled. "We were moving along pretty good.

Even if they hadn't deregulated, we probably would have done pretty well."[38]

The company was not only competing; it was growing in a regulated market. But regulation was soon to become history. The signs were there. In 1962 John Kennedy had been the first president to recommend a reduction in freight transportation regulations. In November 1975, President Gerald Ford called for legislation to reduce regulations and appointed several fans of competition to the Interstate Commerce Commission (ICC).[39]

Opponents of regulation believed it resulted in insufficient competition, which inevitably led to inflated transportation rates. Without the marketplace to determine fair market value, the large trucking companies virtually had a monopoly.

Some fear of what deregulation would bring cropped up among employees at Werner Enterprises. But C. L. had a clear view of the market. "I didn't fight deregulation," he said, "because I knew there was plenty of candy in the candy store. So what we did is we learned how to be efficient, and we [continued to] develop good credit. We were always proud of our credit. We never got behind on anything. We always had good equipment, but we never got in over our heads."[40]

Larsen attested to C. L.'s management style, stellar credit rating, and intelligence. "He's got a brain on him that supercedes about anything," Larsen said. "I always thought a lot of his success was due to his purchasing ability. This has always been a competitive business, but he was much sharper at purchasing than most other companies."[41]

An example of this purchasing acumen was tires. With more than 100 trucks, each utilizing up to 18 tires, the task of tire supply deserved close attention. Interestingly, when it came to tires, not only was C. L. taking advantage of his purchasing abilities; he was also capitalizing on the inefficiency of the larger carriers, Larsen said.

C. L. Werner purchased surplus tires from larger, less efficient trucking companies. His sharp purchasing abilities kept his fleet up to date.

I remember times he used to buy tires off big [trucking] companies like PIE. They're out of business today, but companies like that would overload themselves on tires, and C. L. would pick them up for half price or whatever, "just to bail them out." They needed the money, and C. L. could get it. He was a good trader on equipment too.[42]

Although deregulation didn't officially become the law of the land until 1980, the industry began to loosen up at the end of the 1970s under the Carter administration. For Werner Enterprises, authority was easier and easier to obtain.[43]

Figuring out how to provide the level of service that would secure long-term relationships with shippers was the first challenge. That level of service meant having the equipment to handle these new loads, and getting equipment meant Werner needed capital.

"That was a period of time when there was great opportunity if you had the equipment, because you could go out and solicit business anyplace," said Irving Epstein, who came on as outside counsel to Werner in 1976. "And what C. L. did was he basically hocked himself to his eyeballs to get equipment. It was really a period of time when there was opportunity for anybody who had the fortitude to really gamble and risk everything, and C. L. did that. That really was, I think, the impetus for the beginning of good growth."[44]

C. L. kept reinvesting in Werner Enterprises and protecting the credit rating that had aided the company over the years. "We had a note at the bank for every little thing we had, like a tractor," said then controller, now chief accountant Randy Dickerson. "The security was the tractor and the serial number."[45]

Irving Epstein, an attorney who joined Werner as outside counsel in 1976, said deregulation substantially accelerated Werner's growth. He joined the board of directors in 1986.

But those days were coming to a close as Werner's presence in the trucking sector became more notable. By the end of the 1970s, the company's outstanding credit history bore fruit. "I was able to go out to First Bank in Minnesota and get a $25 million line of credit for equipment at a good rate, and we really started [expanding] our fleet," C. L. said. "I didn't have to deal with the high-cost lenders, the truck fleet leases, and all that. I had cash to go buy trucks, and we bought really good trucks, and we grew this company rapidly."[46]

A Werner truck rolls past the Tarrant County Courthouse in Fort Worth, Texas, in this calendar submission photo.

THE BRAVE NEW WORLD OF TRUCKING
1980–1985

From the time of deregulation in 1980 to the end of 1989, more than 11,000 motor carriers failed. The failures peaked in 1986, when some 1,561 truckers went out of business, or about six every working day.

—Industry Week, 1990

UPON HIS INAUGURAtion in 1976, President Jimmy Carter followed President Ford's lead and pushed efforts to reduce motor carrier regulation. After a series of Interstate Commerce Commission (ICC) rulings that reduced federal oversight of trucking, and after the deregulation of airlines, Congress enacted the Motor Carrier Act (MCA) of 1980.

While consumer advocates, shippers, and small carriers supported deregulation, both the American Trucking Association and the Teamsters Union strongly opposed it. But by this time, an ICC chock full of Ford and Carter appointees was determined to deregulate the industry. Congress stepped in to codify and limit some of the commission changes.[1]

The MCA of 1980 only partially decontrolled trucking, but it substantially freed the industry. It eased the truckers' task of securing a certificate of public convenience and necessity (authority). It also helped eliminate most restrictions on commodities carried, routes taken, and geographic regions served. Truckers could increase or decrease rates from current levels by 15 percent without challenge.[2] Competition made entry into the industry easier for new firms and reduced shipping costs, saving consumers about $5 billion annually.[3]

Deregulation spurred growth at Werner Enterprises and other smaller trucking companies, but the growth came at the expense of the larger carriers. "When deregulation came and authorities were no longer required, the carriers who had built efficiencies into their operations had the advantage and were able to offer shippers far better rates and service, especially on full loads," C. L. Werner told the *World-Herald*.[4]

The 1986 company prospectus reported the benefits of Werner's readiness.

Deregulation of the trucking industry, beginning in 1980, has enabled [Werner Enterprises] to compete for shipments which previously had been carried by the shipper's own trucks or by other carriers. By owning its own standardized late model equipment and employing its own drivers, the company can provide specialized services to meet the requirements of its customers. These services include appointment deliveries, multiple pickups and deliveries, assistance in

---

In 1981 Werner operated 245 tractors and 308 trailers. By 1985 the numbers had jumped to 514 tractors and 1,028 trailers.

loading and unloading, the availability of extra trailers [that] can be placed for the convenience of customers, and sufficient equipment to respond promptly to customers' varying requirements.

Deregulation dealt a blow to many larger carriers that were not prepared. Rich with authority and safe from competition, they had not updated their fleets and facilities during regulation years. "That's why so many of them went bankrupt," C. L. said. "After they wrote the authority off, they didn't have any assets."[5]

Many companies were unable to adapt to the new market, said Bill Legg, an Alex. Brown & Sons analyst and investment banker who specialized in the trucking industry. "Managers who were particularly astute and aggressive, [such as] C. L., J. B. Hunt, and Mike Starnes, were those who emerged successful," Legg said. "They had companies that were well run . . . and unafraid of debt—because trucks were very expensive."[6]

From the start, C. L. had known that trucking was a business of pennies. As a small company duking it out in the days of regulation, he had hustled for every mile and fought for what authority he could get. With his perfect credit rating, he continued to upgrade equipment at every opportunity. So when the market became fair and open, he was already on the move.

"After deregulation we just killed all those [big] companies," C. L. recalled. "We just went in there and killed them. So many of them went broke because they had been charging huge rates."[7]

If outrageous rates weren't enough to precipitate the downfall of numerous carriers, outdated equipment provided the final blow. "They were using 40-foot trailers, and we had 48s," C. L. said. "We were hauling 10 percent more commodity off the bat. But they hadn't had to because they could just keep [smaller] trailers, pay union scale, do whatever they wanted because the shipper had to pay. So, in a sense, the deregulation restructured distribution completely."[8]

C. L. recognized the benefits of deregulation to consumers as well.

It's amazing how fast things changed after deregulation. Before that, the big retail stores had high costs, and they had a distribution system that was very antiquated using union carriers. They were really hurting, and Wal-Mart was

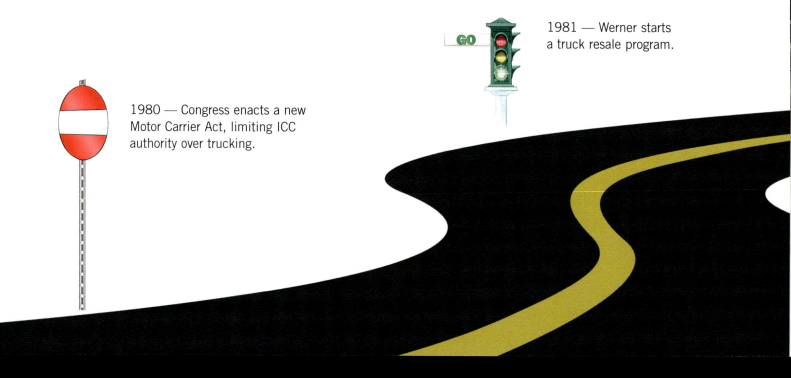

1980 — Congress enacts a new Motor Carrier Act, limiting ICC authority over trucking.

1981 — Werner starts a truck resale program.

CHAPTER FIVE: THE BRAVE NEW WORLD OF TRUCKING

really crimping them because it was utilizing a different distribution system that was available, building the big warehouses.... It just killed the little business guy, but that's progress. People can afford to buy stuff now because prices are less. You can go to Wal-Mart and buy things today for probably less than you paid 25 years ago.[9]

Keeping Morale Alive

While the new deregulated market seemed like a boon to C. L., other team members were not so sure. Drastic rate reductions to lure and retain new customers had been strictly taboo before deregulation, but the playing field had changed. The extreme changes in marketing practices seemed suicidal to C. L.'s right-hand man, dispatcher Jim Larsen. C. L. recalled the pressure customers exerted and Larsen's initial reluctance to cater to their demands.

I don't think Jim really understood what was going to happen with deregulation at first. A customer would say, "Jim, you're going to have to lower your rates 50 cents a mile, or you're not going to keep this business." He would come to me and say, "We're not doing that. They're going to give it to somebody else, but they'll go broke, and we'll get it back." I told him we would be broke before we got it back. I said, "Just handle the business. I'll worry about the rates." We kept Maytag's business, Armstrong Tire, and Firestone. Jim didn't think this would work, but he didn't yet understand the full picture.[10]

Before deregulation, general commodity carriers such as Werner Enterprises were limited to specific routes and rates. As a result, the company had a lot of empty, or "deadhead," back hauls, said Bill Legg. "So what you charged had to include a large percentage of empty miles in order to get your truck back."[11]

C. L. knew he could fill his trucks on return trips and fill them with better freight. By upgrading his cargo, he would boost his margins. "I knew what the market was out there," he recalled. "And I knew what I was going to do with those trucks coming back. They weren't going to haul low-commodity freight now. They were going to haul imported freight, and we were going to make more money."[12]

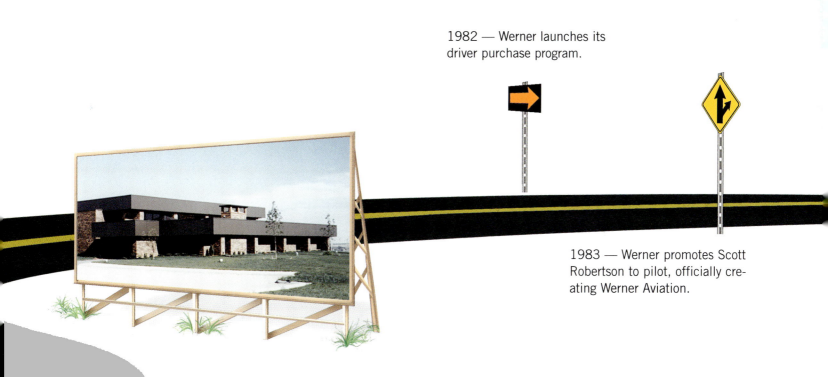

1982 — Werner launches its driver purchase program.

1983 — Werner promotes Scott Robertson to pilot, officially creating Werner Aviation.

Young Blood

By 1980, Gary Werner was playing a crucial role in the company. When he started full-time in 1977, he drove a truck for a few months, and then he was named assistant safety director. Not long after, he became safety director, responsible for all the safety and insurance programs, hiring drivers, and the human resources side of the company.

"I was responsible for all the driver functions back in safety," Gary said. "Verifying employment, hiring the drivers, checking their references, even going out to accident scenes. The basic function of hiring the driver was very much the same as it is today and very important. At that time, we basically just hired experienced drivers because we didn't have the ability to do training back then."[13]

In 1980 Gary was named general manager and was soon immersed in all aspects of the company.

"Of course, we were a lot smaller then, and we didn't have a lot of people," Gary said. "So I was involved in maintenance, purchasing, insurance, safety, and especially marketing."[14]

While Gary served as general manager for two years and then vice president, his younger brother Greg was deeply involved in maintenance. "We had some really good maintenance people," Greg said. "Back then, the trucks were totally different. The life of the trucks was a lot shorter than it is today. We were constantly doing engine overhauls because we kept our trucks a lot longer—up to six years. We didn't have the capital to buy new trucks."[15]

"The engines didn't last as long as they do today, and we kept them longer," Gary added. "So it was much more maintenance work for the same amount of miles. And tires probably ran half the distance or less than they do today."[16]

In 1984, Gary was named president and Greg moved to vice president. But the move was little more than a title change for the brothers. "We were already involved in so many areas of the company," Gary said. "And we had a great, great teacher. C. L. is the best there is. I think I developed a lot in that four-year stretch there. I'd say marketing was the area I grew the most in."[17]

Werner Takes Flight

The company aircraft was vital to Werner's aggressive marketing plan. In 1980, when the race for customers began after deregulation, rarely did a day go by when C. L. or Gary Werner wasn't in the air.

"It was chaotic, but it was exciting as well because there was so much opportunity," Gary said. "But you had a lot of ground to cover in a short amount of time. So you really wanted to make sure you stopped in to see everybody that you possibly could that you wanted to do business with."[18]

But in the midst of all the traveling and courting of new customers, the Werners kept their heads out of the clouds and their feet on the ground.

"We had a good, low cost structure in the late 1970s, and we didn't want to see that deteriorate at all," Gary said. "We'd always given extremely good service, and we wanted to make sure we maintained that service level and didn't let that deteriorate. In 1980, there were so many opportunities that you could have really just shot yourself in the foot."[19]

Many companies did just that. "They lost their focus and lost their direction and tried to grow too fast," Gary said. "Some were going backwards in revenue, and some ended up imploding. So we tried to maintain all of the things that

Werner primarily bought Peterbilt trucks until the early 1980s, when trucks like this Kenworth cabover Aerodyne began rolling onto the company lot.

CHAPTER FIVE: BRAVE NEW WORLD OF TRUCKING 61

Werner encouraged drivers to own their own trucks when the company set up a driver purchase program in the early 1980s.

made the company solid and strong before deregulation and expand upon those."[20]

But the pace was intense, and the company was running lean. C. L. and Gary had their hands full. "We had to catch up and hire some people, but that takes time too," Gary said. "We knew we would have to take time to train new people, so we procrastinated a little bit."[21]

Scott Robertson was one of the new hires in 1980, joining the company as a mechanic earning about $5 an hour. "I thought I'd died and gone to heaven," Robertson said. "I had been pumping gas into airplanes for minimum wage, which was around $2 and some change at the time."[22]

Robertson was a licensed aircraft mechanic but had been unable to find a position that let him flex his skills. He had been dating Gail Werner, who was learning how to fly at the airport where Robertson worked. "You know how to work on planes; maybe you could get a job working on trucks," Gail had suggested.[23]

Robertson knew little about trucks, but he learned quickly. So quickly, in fact, that he caught the eye of the shop foreman, who hired him. "He had to fire the guy running the parts department,"

Robertson recalled. "Once again, I knew nothing about it. But I was young and stupid. I didn't know enough to be scared."[24]

Scott Robertson was on the rise within the Werner operation simply because, like the others, he welcomed change. And it wasn't long before he had another change: he and Gail Werner were married in 1981.

Shortly thereafter, a need arose back in truck maintenance. "The shop foreman decided he was going to start his own trucking company," Robertson said. "So he left to do that, and I was offered the job of shop foreman for truck maintenance."[25]

But Robertson's true love was still flying. Werner aviation had grown to the extent that the company bought a fixed-base operation at the Millard Airport, a small airfield on the southwest side of Omaha. Already a licensed pilot, Robertson didn't hesitate when he saw the opening. He eventually became the manager and president of Werner Aire, which by 2003 would cover all of North America and employ pilots, mechanics, and a small administrative staff.[26]

Building a Used Truck Business

The enormous shift in the dynamics of the trucking industry didn't take long to reach the truck manufacturers. What began as simple economics created a ripple effect that resulted in major advances. "As the distributions changed and the little carriers were becoming big carriers and buying more trucks, the LTL [less than a truckload] people just bought their trucks and ran them forever," C. L. said. "As the truckload industry started growing, the manufacturers really were able to build good trucks [and] engineer good equipment, and there was a huge demand for them. They had to be good, or nobody would buy them. Next thing you know, we had drivetrains running a million miles. We had new synthetic fluids."[27]

The synthetic fluids were a significant breakthrough. Unlike some lubricants of old, the new fluids did not need to be changed until after about 750,000 miles. As a result, Werner's used trucks were nearly new trucks and held a substantial resale value.

"We weren't a big carrier yet, but we were big enough to buy new trucks at a pretty good price," C. L. recalled. "We were running these trucks two years and selling them. We cycled them every two years."[28]

The benefit of turning over trucks at such a rate was twofold. First, purchasing trucks with such frequency made a "bigger buyer" out of Werner, gaining the company pricing that was typically reserved for much larger firms. Second, the resale value of these technologically advanced trucks after just two years was considerable. The system quickly became self-perpetuating. "There

C. L. Werner shows off his custom-built, personalized 1985 Peterbilt show truck, in which he still carries an occasional load.

was a great secondary market for the truckload trucks: the smaller carrier that can't [pay] the big price," C. L. said. "So the buyers are always there. Everybody was buying, so we had a great market, and we were making a lot of money."[29]

Truck dealers took notice of Werner's resale program's success. Rod French, a Kenworth truck dealer in the early 1980s, and Kenworth national sales manager Jim Hebe teamed up to establish what would become a long relationship with Werner.

"Rod and I kind of ganged up to get some business with C. L.," Hebe said. "At the time, C. L. was buying primarily Peterbilt. We decided it was time to send Kenworth his way. So we gathered up our stuff, and we flew out to Omaha. That was really the first time I had done business with C. L. We made a deal for 50 or 100 cabover trucks. Since then we've done quite a bit of business with Werner."[30]

Hebe was impressed with C. L. from the start. "C. L. was interesting," he said. "It was clear that he had a different perspective on the trucks he bought—how long he kept them, how long he ran them, how many miles he put on them, and how he got rid of them. He had a totally different perspective on the management of the assets of his fleet from anybody else in the business."[31]

Hebe realized that C. L.'s specifications for trucks were based not only on quality and resale value. C. L. also considered the interests of his drivers. "He had already come to the realization that you had to keep drivers happy by buying fancy, nice looking, brand-name trucks," Hebe said.[32]

Hebe recalled the strong relationships C. L. cultivated with vendors. "He would drill you," Hebe said. "What's going to happen in three years? Who is the used truck buyer going to be? What are they going to want? But he really made his suppliers part of the business and part of his extended family and friends. That was different from any of the other truckers."[33]

This relationship with vendors allowed for unparalleled latitude and authority in the marketplace. C. L. had enough influence actually to impact the manufacturer's product line. He and Hebe went on a campaign to improve truck specifications. "We came to the conclusion that we could spec trucks with components that could be changed easily when you got rid of them," Hebe said. "We went to the engine manufacturers and got engines that we could buy at lower horsepower and turn up to higher horsepower later in their life. We went to transmission manufacturers and got transmissions that you could run at 10 speeds and convert to 13 speeds when you wanted to trade them off. Those were the kind of things we did to make used trucks a big part of the business."[34]

Hebe attested to C. L.'s vision. "C. L. saw what was going to happen in the used truck business, so he set up his own used truck operation. He saw that coming way before anybody else did, probably because he was much closer to us. We talked an awful lot with him about what we saw happening, and he got a much quicker, much closer perspective on what was going on from our eyes than anybody else did."[35]

Buybacks

One of the ensuing developments that Hebe referred to was manufacturers' buybacks, in which the truck manufacturer, at the time of purchase, agreed to buy back a number of trucks from the buyer after a specified period. But C. L. was uncomfortable allowing the manufacturers to determine the market for used trucks.

"I remember one year I sold C. L. 800 trucks," Rod French said. "I had a postcard to remind myself how many trades we had committed to take. There were many, and we took every one of them. There was another dealer, however, that sold him trucks at the same time. C. L. got hung with 100 of them. When it came time to pony up and pay C. L. for the used ones, the dealer seemed to be oblivious to what they had done. C. L. said at that particular time, 'I'd better be in a position to move my own used trucks.'"[36]

Driver Purchase Program

As the truck resale program matured, Werner added a facet that helped drivers to make the transition to owner-operator. The driver purchase program was a perk to lure the highest-quality drivers who wanted eventually to own trucks. Werner Executive Vice President and Chief Information Officer Bob Synowicki described the benefits the

C. L. Werner, far right, began to ease his sons (from left, Gary, Greg, and Curt) into administrative positions in 1980.

driver purchase program provided to both drivers and the company.

It allows our drivers, if they want, to own their truck. That, in turn, helps us grow as a company; we're going to be attractive to people who maybe can't afford to own their truck right away, but they can come in and drive with us for a while, gain a little bit of cash and equity, and when they feel like they can afford to, we can get them into a truck fairly cheap. It gives us another avenue of growth, and it gives our drivers something that they can shoot for.[37]

Whether through the driver purchase program or resale to smaller carriers, C. L. was certain that Werner's used trucks were the best deal on the market and a tool to strengthen the motor carrier community as a whole. "A small carrier today is 100 to 150 trucks," he said. "It's better off buying a good used truck from us than buying a new one. It helps keep them in business."[38]

According to Greg Werner, company tractors have plush interiors and double-bed bunks. "By providing the latest in equipment, we are able to attract good drivers, and they take pride in their rigs," Greg said. The company itself also took pride in its trucks, diligently providing preventive maintenance in its 13-bay facility.

Stepping Up

Werner Enterprises is full of classic American success stories, of which C. L. is a prime example. Whether his example or his ability to hire exceptional individuals sparked so much success, the fact is he knew his employees were his most valuable asset.

Gene Hansohn found himself knocking on Werner's door after the Chicago-based company he worked for lost several contracts. "A friend of mine was a driver for the Werner family at that time," Hansohn said.[39]

Werner's family environment is what appealed to Hansohn most when he began as a driver in 1976. By 1985, Hansohn had had enough of life on the road.

"One cold day in January I decided this wasn't the life for me anymore," Hansohn said. He blurted to dispatch, "I'm quitting. Period. Getting off the road." But Werner management recognized his value to the company and made him an offer.[40]

Duane Henn, safety director at the time, gave Hansohn three hours to accept a position in his department. "I made a quick call to my wife, who said, 'You don't come home without a job,'" Hansohn recalled. "So that pretty much made up my mind."[41]

Throughout its growth, Werner Enterprises doubled as a breeding ground for individual advancement. While its steady expansion contributed to this ability, the greatest stimulus was the self-development encouraged by the management philosophy: cultivate from the inside. This fearlessness in the face of change had originated with C. L. and had spread throughout Werner Enterprises. From computerization to aviation, people were stepping up and growing in tandem with the company.

The company had been growing steadily. In 1984, Werner ranked number 106 among the nation's trucking firms, based on gross revenues of $53.5 million. In 1985, the company leaped to number 72, with gross revenues of $73.7 million.[42] Yet even that growth would seem small compared to what was to come.

The Henderson, Colorado, terminal was one of three built in 1987 to better service Werner's customers.

WERNER GOES PUBLIC
1986–1989

Long before he ever did it, C. L. had a vision of making Werner Enterprises a public company.

—Rod French, Kenworth dealer
and longtime associate of C. L. Werner

HEADING INTO THE mid-1980s, Werner Enterprises was entering a period of tremendous gain and great risk. Since deregulation in 1980, the trucking industry had undergone systemic and massive changes. Large shippers, such as Sears and other national companies, were beginning to consolidate their shipping. Instead of working with a multiplicity of regional carriers, they began to look for larger trucking companies that could handle all their needs.

At the same time, the national economy entered a period of rapid growth. Throughout the 1980s, interest rates remained relatively low, unemployment was under control, and corporate America fared well. The stock market responded to these conditions and rose steadily throughout the early and mid-1980s. This boom, although small by 1990s standards, fueled a huge wave of mergers and acquisitions throughout American industry. It also created the perfect conditions for entrepreneurs who wanted to take their companies public.

These two factors—a consolidation in its industry and an intense IPO (initial public offering) market—combined to make the trucking industry "hot" by investment banker standards. Regional carriers such as Werner and its competitors wanted access to the plentiful capital available through the stock markets to fuel the rapid growth they would need in the changed world of trucking. This need was more than a matter of ambition or even personal enrichment. It was a matter of survival, especially for Werner, which still carried a significant amount of debt on its balance sheet.

Fortunately for Werner Enterprises, C. L. Werner had positioned the company well. Werner had a fleet of up-to-date trucks and solid relationships with its drivers. Unlike many of its competitors, Werner owned its own trucks, and the company counted among its assets almost 500 tractor rigs, the average age of which was less than two years.[1] The company's marketing department also commanded respect throughout the industry. Werner boasted a two-to-one ratio of trailers to tractors to accommodate the needs of high-volume shippers, and it worked closely with customers on multiple pickups and deliveries of partial loads.[2]

"A key element of the company's emphasis on service is its strong commitment to accommodating the individualized requirements of the company's shippers," declared the 1986 annual report, noting that in the last five years, Werner

---

Werner Enterprises goes public on Nasdaq in June 1986, and its first annual report is presented to its stockholders.

had never lost a shipper that accounted for revenue in excess of $500,000 per year.³

For all of these reasons, Werner Enterprises was a promising company in the eyes of investment bankers, which suited C. L. Werner. He had, after all, always hoped to take his company public. All that remained was finding the right partners and the right situation to introduce Werner Enterprises to the public.

The Dance Begins

Early in 1986, various investment banking companies approached Werner, offering to take the company public. Irving Epstein, who had provided outside counsel for Werner "since the days when C. L. had 10 trucks," recalled the environment as Werner and Wall Street courted each other.

"The brokerage houses wanted to issue IPOs," Epstein said. "You had a period where the investment bankers were looking for product. It's good for the entrepreneur, but it's also good for the investment banker. All of a sudden, trucking became fashionable. There were other companies going public, and here was a good candidate in Werner, and we went through a mating dance because we had different investment bankers coming forward."⁴

Curt Werner accompanied his father on various trips to New York and saw for the first time how the public financial markets operated. "At the time, I was in my early 20s," Curt said. "It was such a learning experience to see how Wall Street works. That was just incredible."⁵

As president of the company, Gary Werner was very involved in investor relations. He and C. L. worked hard to prove themselves on Wall Street. After the offering, they spent a great deal of time visiting shareholders and doing presentations. "They just wanted to see management and feel comfortable with the company," Gary recalled. "We had to build trust and show that Werner Enterprises was here to stay."⁶

His brother Greg noted the skill with which his brother and father took the company public.

Gary and C. L. went out and talked with passion on the business, and they know the industry so well that it made people comfortable. They thought, "Yeah, these guys are going to do what they say they're going to do." They were well-grounded, they didn't overpromise, and they

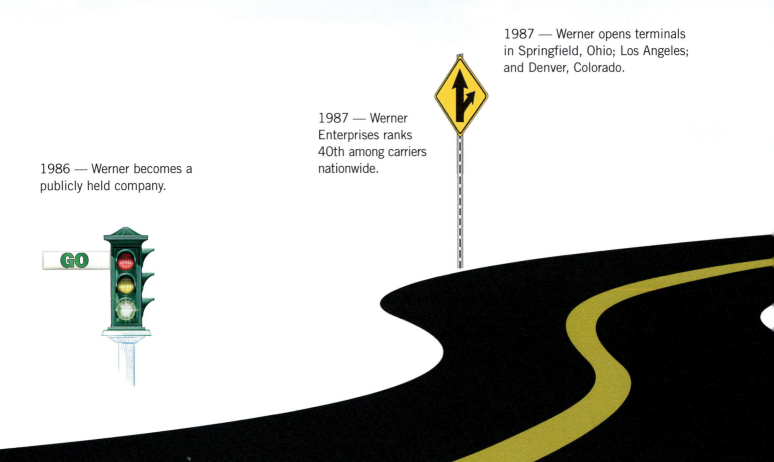

1986 — Werner becomes a publicly held company.

1987 — Werner Enterprises ranks 40th among carriers nationwide.

1987 — Werner opens terminals in Springfield, Ohio; Los Angeles; and Denver, Colorado.

CHAPTER SIX: WERNER GOES PUBLIC

didn't overreach. They earned a tremendous amount of respect within our industry and from Wall Street. Gary, especially, has always been very good at asking the questions, the what-ifs.[7]

After meeting with several investment houses, C. L. chose Alex. Brown & Sons to underwrite the company's offering. Brown, in turn, brought legal counsel Piper Marbury on board, and Arthur Andersen was retained to put the company's books in order and provide forecasting.

Bill Legg, an investment banker and former research analyst with Alex. Brown, said his company was interested in Werner because of its position in the market and the sheer opportunity of the truckload market. After deregulation, Legg said, truckload carriers could realize a higher return on their investment because they could eliminate empty miles.[8]

The press took an increased interest in Werner Enterprises after the company went public. C. L. Werner posed with his children (from left), Gary, Greg, Gail, and Curt, for this 1986 photo for the *Omaha World-Herald Magazine of the Midlands*.

1988 — C. L. Werner is named chairman of the Nebraska Motor Carriers Association's board of directors.

"The truckload part of the trucking industry really had its 15 minutes of fame postderegulation," Legg said.

Deregulation created an environment where the aggressive and the smart could grow their businesses. The business just boomed. We took a lot of the companies public ... the ones that had the combination of good management and the aggressiveness to take on the debt to build the company.

You have to take the debt on first before you can pay it down because you take on the debt to build the company, which shows Wall Street that you're an attractive investment. The valuation goes up to the point where you then can pay down the debt with dollars that are less expensive than your debt.[9]

By early summer 1986, everything was in place. In June, Werner sold two million shares of stock on the over-the-counter (OTC) market. The shares had an opening price of $17 and rose to $22 within the first three months.[10] C. L. Werner and his children remained the company's largest private shareholders.

This influx of capital would allow Werner to greatly increase its growth rate, according to chief accountant Randy Dickerson.

We were basically growing at a consistent rate, putting money back into the company as we were making it. When we got to the point where we could really see there was a marketplace, that's really why we [decided to go] public. Going public generated immense dollars, and those dollars let us really grow at a phenomenal rate.[11]

Deregulation had created a market that made it easier for transportation companies to go public, and many did. "As time went on, we've really gotten out of that government environment, more into a free market–type economy where it's just like any other business, taking competition and running with it," Dickerson said.[12]

A Strong Ending

The influx of almost $16 million of capital was exactly what Werner needed, and the company went on a dizzying growth spurt. "Ironically, it took 10 tough years to grow to 125 rigs," C. L. told the *World-Herald* in October 1986. "Last June [when we went public], we added 125 power units and hired 150 drivers in a 30-day period."[13]

Using the money raised from the initial public offering, Werner also began to build the necessary infrastructure to handle ever larger contracts from national shippers. Now Werner could achieve economies of scale and drive down the cost of every load.

"In 1986, when we went public, we were able to get a clean balance sheet and start growing again," said Bob Synowicki, executive vice president and chief information officer. "Back in 1987, it wasn't unusual for a company like Sears to have 300 trucking companies hauling freight for them. As some of these [trucking] companies began to grow, the Searses of the world decided, 'Hey, I don't want to deal with 300 trucking companies anymore. I want to deal with 10.'"[14]

Werner's business took off in the late 1980s, keeping the company's offices busier than ever. From left are the driver payroll department, the computer room, the marketing department, the operations department, and Gary Werner's office.

CHAPTER SIX: WERNER GOES PUBLIC

The trend toward fewer, but larger, shipping companies became known as the "core carrier concept," and companies like Werner, willing to gamble on rapid growth, stood to benefit a great deal. An article in *Industry Week* magazine noted that Werner Enterprises was among a small group of companies that fit the core carrier model.

"Of the more than 40,000 trucking companies operating for hire in the U.S., there are only a handful of first-rate, premium-quality, customer-driven truckload motor carriers," the article declared.

> *Such carriers as J. B. Hunt, Builders Transport, Schneider National, M. S. Carriers, Munson Transportation, and Werner Enterprises are among the few firms truly aiming at—and capable of reaching—zero defects in transportation. These companies are growing at 20 percent to 30 percent annually because they can help industry reduce inventories and lower costs.*[15]

The article went on to identify the challenges facing core carriers. Chief among them were a shortage of "human resources," or drivers, and market fragmentation among the major carriers. No truckload carrier had more than a 3 percent market share, and turnover was widespread. A *Forbes* profile of J. B. Hunt, the industry leader, provided a perfect example of these forces at work. In 1987, the company experienced a 100 percent turnover among its drivers and had less than a 3 percent market share.[16]

Werner operated 632 tractors in 1986. By 1991 it had acquired close to 2,500.[17] "Finding drivers was probably our most challenging issue at the time," Gary said. "The trucking industry was growing so fast during the late 1980s that driver shortages were pretty much across the board. Everybody was scrambling for talent. It was a constant struggle."[18]

Werner dealt with these pressures by growing its way past them. In 1987, noting that "as is typical of the...trucking industry, the company experiences significant driver turnover," Werner Enterprises grew to 995 drivers, an increase of almost 50 percent in a single year.[19] That year, sales jumped from $73.7 million to $94.4 million.[20]

Werner also set out on an ambitious, IPO-fueled building campaign. In 1987, three terminal facilities opened. In central Ohio, a 7,000-square-foot facility was leased while the company built a 20,400-square-foot terminal in Springfield. The Springfield terminal was expected to open in 1988 and to cost $750,000. On the West Coast, Werner bought a 15,000-square-foot dispatch and maintenance facility in Los Angeles. And finally, in Denver, Werner leased a 9,800-square-foot facility while a new terminal was built.[21] These strategically located terminals would greatly expand Werner's reach and efficiency for national routes.

This growth spurt was an exciting vindication of years of hard work, both for Werner and for C. L. In 1987, Werner Enterprises was named number 40 among all carriers nationwide and was among the top 10 truckload carriers nationally. Then in September 1988, C. L. Werner was named chairman of the Nebraska Motor Carriers Association's board of directors. Two months later, he sat for an interview with *Nebraska Trucker* magazine and reflected on the previous five years of fast growth, telling a reporter that as many as 200 trucks a day rumbled through the gates of the Omaha terminal.

"I attribute our success in the Midwest to our central location, which allows us to service all parts of the U.S.; to the good Interstate system; and to all

the strong work ethic of the people in this area," C. L. said. "Deregulation gave us the authority to haul all commodities in all the states. Now we have the open market, and it's been very good to us."[22]

By the end of the year, Werner was ready to close the books on a record-breaking performance. That year, revenue increased an amazing 47 percent to $139 million, and income jumped by 34 percent. Also, the company completed a secondary stock offering.

"We have proven our ability to expand the company at a steady, consistent rate through good and bad economic times," C. L. Werner wrote in the annual report. "We expect our revenue growth to continue at 20 to 25 percent a year."[23]

Nevertheless, the challenges for the years ahead were clear. Some of them were familiar, such as the shortage of qualified drivers. Werner, which went to great lengths to keep its drivers satisfied, suffered relatively little from this problem, and by 1988 the company had almost 1,500 drivers.

Meeting the Market

Other challenges, however, were new. The recent deregulation had invited newcomers into the industry. As C. L. pointed out, "Deregulation allowed virtually anyone who could afford the price of a truck to start a trucking company."[24] Furthermore, the addition of 48- and 53-foot trailers reduced the number of loads available by increasing the carrying capacity of each truck. This was good short-term news for shippers, who were saving freight costs, but bad news for trucking companies, who were watching their margins tumble into single-digit percentages.

Ultimately, C. L. predicted, this glut of capacity would trigger a familiar cycle: Prices would bottom out, and inefficient, unprofitable carriers would go out of business. As a result, rates would eventually drift back up, allowing companies like Werner to update their fleets once again.

"We are well positioned as one of the largest, most innovative companies in the emerging truckload group," C. L. said. "Our commitment to our customers, our premium equipment and our national freight set us apart from our competition. . . . We feel the future is bright for Werner Enterprises."[25]

This opinion was widely shared throughout the industry and the tight-knit group of analysts who followed trucking company stocks. In 1988, *Forbes* magazine ran a quick poll of analysts' picks for truck company stocks. Werner Enterprises made the short list.

> *Transportation analyst John Larkin of Alex. Brown likes Omaha-based Werner Enterprises, Inc., a large truckload carrier that he compares with J. B. Hunt Transport Services, the acknowledged star of the field. Some of the reasons Werner has built an impressive reputation among shippers, according to Larkin: a sizable fleet of new, well-maintained, reliable equipment; strong financials; ability to exchange data with customers electronically and so cut down on paperwork; a good record for on-time pickups and deliveries. Werner's roughly 15 percent operating margins should give it significant flexibility to meet pricing competition.*[26]

By 1989, Werner Enterprises could look back on a satisfying decade. Despite the pressures on its industry, from both within and without, the company had maintained a blistering

Werner's IPO raised the capital the company needed to handle contracts from national shippers, keeping the wheels of Werner Enterprises rolling smoothly.

CHAPTER SIX: WERNER GOES PUBLIC

rate of growth. In 1989, the company reported an impressive 38 percent increase in revenue, to $191.4 million, and income jumped 33 percent.[27] And there was still plenty of opportunity for growth. The for-hire truckload market was estimated at $15 billion to $20 billion annually, and the market was still fragmented. In that year's annual report, C. L. Werner pointed out that the top 10 truckload carriers held only 13 percent of the total market. This left "significant room for consolidation."[28] This consolidation would be matched by the continuing consolidation by shippers, which were turning to fewer truckload carriers.

"Werner Enterprises is one of a handful of carriers positioned to service these shippers," C. L. said.

Our number one priority is to provide outstanding customer service. The operating philosophy of Werner Enterprises is to be flexible by tailoring our business structure to the needs of our shippers. This approach has been, and will continue to be, a significant contributing factor to our success.[29]

By the end of the decade, the Werner Enterprises of 10 years before would have been hardly recognizable. The company owned almost 1,800 tractors, employed 2,251 drivers, and had facilities in Omaha, Ohio, and Los Angeles. Werner also leased facilities in Denver and Dallas. The company had recently bought land in both cities and planned to open new terminals within a year. In 10 years, it had become a public company and one of the leading truckload carriers in the United States.

"In 1989, the company was rapidly growing," recalled Vice President and Chief Financial Officer John Steele. "C. L. had a need to add some more financial talent. He made me an offer I couldn't refuse, and I came aboard in 1989."[30]

C. L. Werner's distinctive management style and the risks he had taken to build his company had paid off. Werner Enterprises, with revenues of $251 million in 1989, had become a very successful carrier indeed.

Above: Vice President, Treasurer, and CFO John Steele joined Werner in 1989, recognizing the company as a flagship firm.

Below: Werner Enterprises grew at a faster rate thanks to its small fleet of aircraft. C. L. stepped off this new plane in 1986.

Steele already had been auditing the Werner account for a few years for Arthur Andersen. "I had served several trucking clients [for Arthur Andersen], and I was aware of Werner Enterprises," he said. "I requested the opportunity to work on the Werner Enterprises account because it was a flagship, successful, growing trucking company."[31]

The move was a smart one from a financial expert's point of view. "Werner has always been a pretty conservative company," Steele said. "It's not a highly leveraged company. C. L. is a fairly conservative person when it comes to fiscal management. He doesn't want to take financial risks that could bankrupt the company. That's not to say he isn't a risk taker. He takes calculated business risks and is one of those people who has more common sense in the business world than anybody I've ever known."[32]

Heading into the 1990s, industry watchers were predicting changes ahead, especially in the manufacturing sector. Throughout the 1980s, American manufacturing had been undergoing a wrenching self-examination provoked by overseas manufacturing competition, mostly Japanese. Throughout the 1980s, Japanese automobile and electronics manufacturers had steadily taken market share in America. These Japanese manufacturing firms, such as Honda and Sony, were faster, more efficient, had better quality, and offered products at better prices.

By the beginning of the 1990s, however, the American companies were beginning to catch up, both by exporting manufacturing overseas and by overhauling their operations. Rapid-response, flexible manufacturing philosophies, such as just-in-time and lean manufacturing, were beginning to make inroads into American factories.

The effect on the transportation industry would be profound, according to *Industry Week*. Trucking companies would have to become "premium" carriers to survive, able to deliver goods flawlessly to factories that relied on them for continuing operation.

"In 1987 the average shipper still used 80 carriers, but projections show that by 1990, the number will drop to 60, and by 1995 to fewer than 50," wrote reporter Brian Moskal.

A carrier-industry concentration is taking place as shippers move toward the use of fewer carriers," says Arnaud J. Wilson [a manager with A. T. Kearney]. *"When it ends, all carriers will be in one of two categories—a major player or a niche/flex player that picks up the slack. Right now, many are in the middle and will have to make a decision soon about their future.*[33]

Another analyst, Patrick Bryne, partner and director of transportation consulting at Ernst & Whinney, predicted that the truckload market would shake down to about 30 well-known companies by the mid-1990s. These would most likely be companies that were already established, partially because the competition was so fierce and partly because, since the Black Monday stock market crash of 1987, IPO dollars had dried up.

"For shippers to regard a trucking company as a core carrier, the carrier must be able to grow its asset base—tractors, trailers, drivers, and facilities—as well as manage that growth to provide high service at low cost," *Industry Week* said.

"With margin-erosion problems among numerous carriers, with all of the leveraged-buyout financing activity we have seen in the truckload sector, and with a number of truckload bankruptcies, it occurs to us there are only a relatively few carriers who meet a shipper's core-carrier standards and are in a strong position to capture customer and market share," believes John G. Larkin, trucking analyst with Alex. Brown & Sons.[34]

Werner Enterprises was determined to be among the winners. The company had spent the last decade positioning itself for just such a challenge. It had a new fleet, loyal drivers, an advanced communications system, national scope, and management willpower.

"The future is not without challenges and factors that are difficult to control," C. L. said in 1989. "However, we firmly believe that Werner Enterprises is uniquely positioned to manage these changes. We are confident about the future."[35]

By the end of 1993, Werner Enterprises had 3,000 trucks on the road, including dedicated, temperature-controlled, regional short-haul, flatbed, and dry vans.

TRAVELING A BUMPY ROAD
1990–1992

Probably more than 80 percent of the nation's trucking industry is caught in an economic vise. As rates have remained the same or dropped, costs have risen.

— Industry Week, 1990

THE EARLY YEARS OF THE 1990s saw a technological revolution that changed the face of the world. Instant communications, rapid technological advances, and lightning-fast Internet connections brought global issues into our living rooms. We watched "smart bombs" drop in the Persian Gulf War and witnessed a deadly firestorm at a religious-sect compound in Waco, Texas.

At the start of the decade, the economy was heading into a deep and widening recession. A bailout of failed savings and loans was costing taxpayers billions, and unemployment was on its way to 7.8 percent in 1992.

But at Werner Enterprises, there was no recession. While many factories were laying off workers, not one Werner Enterprises job was eliminated. In fact, at the height of the recession, in 1990, Werner's firm increased its fleet by 550 tractors and hired drivers to fill them. The year also marked the grand opening of a company store that sold everything from Wrangler jeans and Werner jackets to corncob jelly and teddy bears. The company added a terminal in Atlanta and reported record revenues and earnings. Operating revenues rose 31 percent, from $191.4 million in 1989 to $251.6 million. By 1990 Werner Enterprises was one of the five largest of 30,000 truckload carriers in the United States.[1]

Reduce Speed Ahead

The trucking industry suffered lean periods in the early 1990s. In August 1990 Iraqi dictator Saddam Hussein invaded neighboring Kuwait, which led to the Persian Gulf War. Fuel prices had already spiked dramatically. On December 29, 1989, the price per gallon of diesel fuel increased 12 cents. By January 2, 1990, diesel fuel prices were nearly 30 cents a gallon higher. In 1991, with the war in full swing, the economy slowed due to inordinately high petroleum costs. Consequently, truckload carriers' margins suffered, and it seemed impossible to recover from the high cost of fuel.[2]

Analysts predicted hard times for highly leveraged companies, but the very frugality that some criticized Werner for turned out to be a lifesaver for the truckload carrier. In response to industry trends, Werner made the decision to actually slow its growth. "We will be less aggressive this year," C. L. Werner wrote in the 1990 annual report. "This will help Werner maintain one of the strongest balance sheets in the industry and limit our risk in the event of an economic recession."[3]

Werner's company newsletter, *The Enterpriser,* was chock full of tips and illustrations to remind drivers to travel safely.

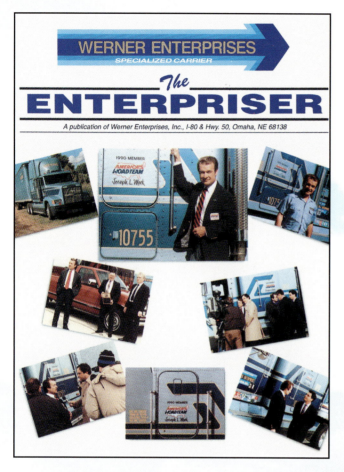

A 1990 company newsletter, *The Enterpriser,* read, "Higher prices for diesel fuel and a sick economy [are] accelerating the shakeout in the trucking industry. The strongest truck companies are going to get a lot stronger, and the weak ones are going to get a lot weaker, if they survive at all."[4]

Industry Week called for more consolidations, especially among the "children of deregulation. These are the carriers born just before or after deregulation in 1980. It was easy for them to enter the trucking market because they didn't need the capital outlays required by the less than truckload carriers to establish terminals. Now they are finding that the easy market entry is a two-way street and exit is just as easy."[5]

Shipper Shortage

The early 1990s also brought a carrier-to-shipper imbalance. "The truck industry has more capacity to haul freight than there is demand," reported *Industry Week.* In 1980, 17,000 compa-

The fall 1990 *Enterpriser* cover touted the company's honors.

1990 — Werner receives the Golden Spike from the Western Council of Greater Omaha Chamber of Commerce and makes *Forbes'* list of "200 Best Small Companies."

1990 — Werner increases its fleet by 550 tractors and opens a new terminal in Atlanta.

1992 — Werner enters the dedicated, regional, and refrigerated truckload freight markets.

CHAPTER SEVEN: TRAVELING A BUMPY ROAD

nies provided transportation for shippers. By 1990 that number had more than doubled while the number of shippers remained static. Shippers, looking for a competitive advantage through wiser use of trucking services, continued the trend toward reducing the number of carriers that handled their freight.[6]

Only Werner, J. B. Hunt, Schneider National, and a handful of others had the capacity to meet these shippers' needs. These top carriers began to grow at rates of 20 to 30 percent annually, based on their proven abilities to reduce industry inventories and thus cut costs.[7]

As shippers continued to move toward just-in-time production, the demand for premium transportation services exploded. The need for core carriers far exceeded their number or capacity.[8]

Werner Enterprises fit the bill as a core carrier. John G. Larkin, a trucking analyst with Alex. Brown and Sons, pointed to factors that would contribute to the attrition rate, leaving only a few elite carriers to handle this new demand. "With margin erosion problems among numerous carriers, with all of the leveraged-buyout financing activity we have seen in the truckload sector, and

The pages of *The Enterpriser* devoted plenty of space to Werner's top priority of safe driving.

1992 — Satellite communication equipment is installed in the company's entire fleet.

1993 — Werner makes an additional secondary offering.

with a number of truckload bankruptcies, it occurs to us there are only a relatively few carriers who meet a shipper's core-carrier standards and are in a strong position to capture customer and market share," Larkin said.[9]

Werner had also anticipated a shortage of human resources—namely drivers and managers. Industrywide, revenues weren't substantial enough to attract top professional managers, and most companies couldn't afford to develop entry-level would-be managers.[10] In comparison, the "flashy" technology/computer industry gobbled up ambitious managers.

But Werner was positioned extremely well in comparison to its competition.

When the marketplace downshifted, quality managers were already in place at Werner. In fact, in 1991 Gary Werner was promoted to vice chairman and Bob Synowicki was promoted to vice president and CFO. Werner also had one of the best driver recruiting and training programs in the business.[11] But drivers weren't the only ones being trained.

Building the Team

By 1990, Werner Enterprises had taken a new approach to hiring. When the company started a program to pump new, college-educated blood through the veins of the company, Vice President of Operations Guy Welton was one of the first. He believed hiring college-educated people opened new doors.

"A lot of potential candidates out there may not have considered a career in transportation," said Welton, who started as a dispatcher. "They may not have a whole lot of experience in transportation, but we can teach them that. And if they've got the desire and motivation to contribute and to improve themselves, it's going to be good for both the employee and the company."[12]

Left: By 1991 Werner Enterprises had been on the road for 35 years.

Below: Driver training sessions are an integral part of Werner's ongoing state-of-the-art safety program.

CHAPTER SEVEN: TRAVEL

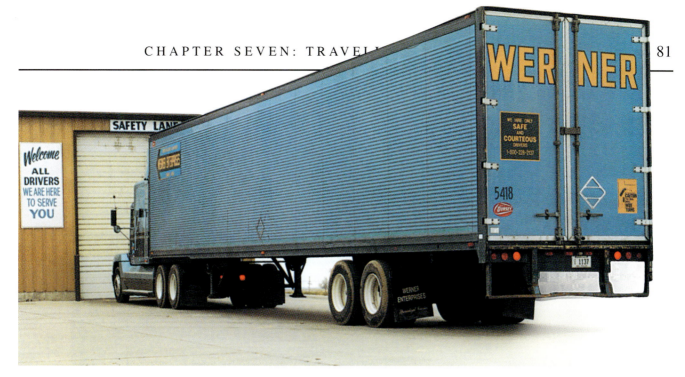

Werner's cross-training program became an efficient model for moving employees across divisions. Welton worked in marketing for four years after a year as dispatcher. From there, he moved into a business improvement position, interacting with all the departments.

"It is very beneficial to cross-train people, move them around," Welton said. "I got a very good idea of how we operated as an entire company. You can't have boundaries around your own department and just worry about yourselves. You've got to look at what is best for the overall company. We're homegrown. We don't like to look for employees outside of the company now. We like people inside to prove themselves and move up the ranks."[13]

New Divisions

Slow growth in hard times paid off, as the 1992 annual report noted: "Taking our cue from the economy and our own internal observations, we used the first half of fiscal 1992 to further consolidate a strong financial position by paying down debt. Our debt-to-equity ratio as of February 1992 was 11 percent—one of the lowest in the trucking industry."

Of course slow growth didn't mean no growth. After much research, C. L. decided to enter new facets of the market in 1992—the regional, dedicated, and refrigerated truckload freight arenas.

The regional market was a boon to drivers who wanted to be home every night. They drove

Above: All trucks must pass through Werner's safety lane before heading for the open road.

Below: The cover of the Werner Enterprises 1992 annual report

shorter distances and stuck to metropolitan areas. Through Werner's dedicated fleet services, it began contracting with companies to provide their total logistics and transportation requirements.

Larry Williams, an account executive at the time, was selected to get the regional division up and running.

"When C. L. asked me to start regional fleets, he didn't sit down and say, 'Here's what you're going to do, here's how you're going to do it, and this is what I want to see today and tomorrow and the next day.' All he said was, 'We want you to take this concept and develop it. You're on your own.' There is no micromanaging at Werner. The pressure of management is self-exerted because of the leeway and the expectations that you put on yourself to please the Werner family."[14]

Larger truckload carriers increasingly began to see potential in providing dedicated contract carriage in the 1990s. The industry trend meant more than simply committing a predetermined number of trucks and drivers to a customer. The service provided complete transportation management services for shippers, allowing them to focus more closely on their primary business.

The move would eventually prove profitable for Werner Enterprises. Meanwhile, its biggest competitors included leasing companies, such as Ryder.[15]

"Using dedicated service follows the trend for customers to outsource their transportation services," Curt Werner told the *Midlands Business Journal*. "We either take over the existing fleet or put in our own equipment and handle their transportation. It lets our customers focus on what they do best, which is typically manufacturing a product."[16]

The dedicated market was a $17 billion industry nationwide when Werner entered it. "Years ago," Curt explained, "a transportation company picked something up from point A and delivered it to point B. Today customers are asking us to participate in their total transportation needs. That may mean warehousing, leasing trucks and trailers to them, handling multiple

The Nebraska State Patrol and former Governor Ben Nelson pose with police dog Kastor, purchased with funds donated by Werner Enterprises.

facilities, or doing less-than-a-load hauling. It's a true partnership."[17]

The dedicated-service concept stemmed from a philosophy known as "total logistics," which emerged in the early 1990s. The idea was for companies to outsource most or all of their shipping to transportation specialists that could offer not only the economies of scale of a large carrier but the expertise that comes from years of trucking.

"Customers started to realize it was more cost efficient to utilize companies that owned assets to haul for them," said Vice President of Dedicated Operations Marty Nordlund. "They are saving insurance costs, and the price of equipment and fuel. Everybody started to focus more on their core competencies, and they decided trucking wasn't theirs."[18]

Companies competing in the dedicated market were either asset-based or non-asset-based. Asset-based companies, like Werner, provided tractors, trailers, and related hardware as well as transportation management services. Non-asset-based companies simply provided logistics services.[19]

"Our advantage is that we can provide our own equipment in 48 states and draw upon our trucking background to handle the customer's transportation needs," Curt Werner said. "Non-asset companies have to broker their freight needs to carriers. We have more flexibility and availability, which is a big advantage in the marketplace." The dedicated division catered to customers who were losing money by owning their own fleets, Williams said. "There was just no way they could be making money because of the upkeep and the drivers and the fuel. So trucking companies like Werner stepped in and took care of it for them."[20]

Upon entering the refrigerated market, Werner became the largest carrier offering the service. "Our customers had been asking for temperature-controlled service and had offered to participate in some partnerships with us," C. L. said.[21]

Additionally, some long-haul freight lines were eroding due to rail competition, and refrigerated service offered another angle to compete.[22]

The fragmented refrigerated market consisted of an abundance of smaller carriers. At the time, the majority of refrigerated carriers generated less than $30 million annually, C. L. said. Fewer than 10 of them brought in more than $100 million. But Werner had 150 refrigerated trailers running in its first year in the market, and by the end of 1993 it ran more than 400 trailers.[23]

What to Haul

Although located in the heart of the beef capital of the world, Werner had no intention of basing its temperature-control business around hauling meat. "We'll haul meat, but we won't make it the basis of our system," C. L. said.[24]

Born and raised in the Great Plains and having built his business there, C. L. understood the special nature of the meat trade. "Remember," he cautioned, "for years all our local competition was from refrigerated carriers that depended on meat packers. We even tried it once in 1971 with 15 trucks. We gave up our concentration on meat hauling after six months. Some of our competitors lasted longer, but most of them are gone now. Frozen foods and prepared convenience products are the blocks for building a refrigerated carrier."[25]

Werner differentiated itself with its unloading procedures, put in place to assure quality and reward drivers. "One of our goals is to get every tractor back under load on the same day of the trip," C. L. said. "We have an internal incentive to get tractors moving again. If a load is off a trailer by 1 P.M. and we cannot dispatch the driver to another load that same day, we pay waiting time. That does two things. Paying for waiting keeps our drivers happy because they get something for sitting still. Before we instituted this policy, drivers didn't make any money for waiting. Operations personnel, specifically dispatchers, have an economic reason to get the truck reloaded. Everybody knows that a parked truck costs [the company], but somehow knowledge that the company is paying the driver for sitting still seems to be more of a motivating factor," he told *Refrigerated Transport*.[26]

While these procedures proved effective in increasing customer satisfaction, they simultaneously addressed driver retention. "Failure to get unloaded on the same day usually is caused by a holdup at the receiver," C. L. said. "When we started paying drivers for waiting, the loads going to troublesome receivers really began to stick out.

The cover of the 1991 annual report portrayed Werner rolling past a sparkling skyline. Werner reported record revenues and earnings despite the challenging year, which included war and an economic slowdown.

The result has been a concerted effort to work harder to get trailers unloaded promptly."[27]

Werner decided to start its temperature-control division from scratch rather than purchase an existing operation from another carrier. "We could design the equipment we wanted, which gives us the capability to start life with new, high-cube trailers built with proven thermal integrity," C. L. said.[28]

Director of maintenance at the time of the initial equipment purchase, Dwayne Haug, said the standard refrigeration unit then was the Carrier Transicold Ultra Units equipped with R-22 refrigeration gas. "We plan to keep these trailers in service five to seven years," Haug said. "Our trade cycle is based on our use of equipment and its potential resale value. These trailers should be worth quite a lot to a buyer at the end of seven years. We chose R-22 as the responsible thing to do for the company as well as for the resale of the trailers."[29]

"This equipment is a cooperative effort between the company and our suppliers," Haug continued. "We have a number of people on our staff who have worked for refrigerated carriers. We used that experience along with careful consultation with Wabash National to design the most modern refrigerated trailers on the road."[30]

Above: Driver Jeff Kreutztrager works with the Qualcomm communication system, which provides Werner drivers continuous contact with dispatch and communication with family via e-mail.

Below left: The Qualcomm communication unit was installed on board every Werner truck in 1992.

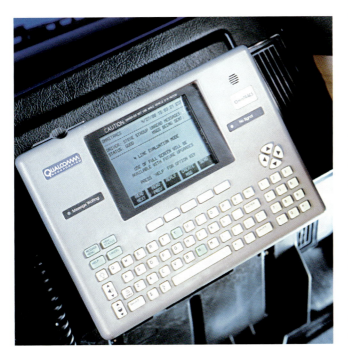

The Qualcomm System

Werner had long been aware that efficiency and safety have an intertwined relationship in the motor carrier industry. The adoption of the Qualcomm system, a satellite-based, fleetwide communication system, was born out of this marriage of efficiency and safety.

In September 1992 Werner Enterprises signed a three-year contract valued at more than $12 million with Qualcomm Inc. for its OmniTRACS mobile communications system. The system's two-way message and position location capabilities allowed the carrier to maintain real-time communications and track its fleet of more than 2,700 dry vans and flatbeds.[31]

"With cutthroat competition and a shortage of good drivers, it is no surprise that terminal managers seek a more dependable way to find freight," reported the *Journal of Commerce* shortly after the contract was signed. "The result has been an increasing number of trucking companies willing to fork over millions of dollars for new high-tech machinery to track their trucks."[32]

Priced at roughly $4,000 a truck in 1992, the system offered communication by keyboard and phone lines. Lee Easton, vice president of management information systems for Werner, explained the basic facets of the system. "The Qualcomm system consists of two different parts. One is messaging, like e-mail. We send the driver various information, such as load information or payroll information. The second part is what we call position histories, location of the trucks. These are given to us by latitude and longitude."[33]

"It opens up a whole new world," said George Weller, director of fleet operations for Werner at the time. Weller said he slept better at night "not playing the guessing games" to find each of the company's 2,700 trucks. The system allowed better planning of freight shipments, more consistency, better driver treatment, flexibility to contact drivers, and ability to change routes instantly. "There are all kinds of advantages here," Weller said.[34]

The Qualcomm system was basically a global positioning system. Easton compared it to the cheaper systems available to the public for personal use. "You can buy these very cheaply for a couple hundred dollars," he said. "Fishermen or hunters would buy them so they wouldn't get lost out in the woods. That is the basis of it."[35]

But Werner's system went far beyond that. "We calculate the driver's moving time, his logging, his on duty/off duty, his on duty/not driving, and

Inset this page: Lee Easton, vice president of Management Information Systems for Werner, said the satellite communication system allows the company to locate a truck on the road at any time.

Inset opposite: Vice President of Safety Duane Henn said the system saves lives and deters theft.

CHAPTER SEVEN: TRAVELING A BUMPY ROAD

his sleeper berth time," Easton said. "We can determine how far and how long the driver has driven. There are certain hours-of-service guidelines drivers have to follow. They cannot drive for longer than 10 hours in any day. They cannot be on duty more than 15 hours in one day. They cannot have a combined 70 hours in an eight-day period."[36]

Curt Werner added, "When a truck begins moving, we literally know how many miles it will be from point A to point B, and it's all compiled in our computers, and we can dispatch our drivers accordingly."[37]

Forever safety conscious, C. L. reiterated the contribution the system made in protecting drivers. "It has been very, very important," he said. "We are the only trucking company in the country that monitors drivers' hours electronically real time here in dispatch, and that's very big. Basically, we're set up on a 70-hour, eight-day schedule for a driver, and as they drive across from city to city, it keeps track of every minute that they're driving."[38]

The Qualcomm system also deterred theft and saved drivers' lives. "We have had equipment stolen, and we were able to track it by the satellite position history," Duane Henn said. "It actually saved a driver's life. He had stopped on a side street to make a delivery, and as he was sitting in the cab, a group walked by and actually fired a gun through the side window. [A bullet] entered his neck and nicked his carotid artery. The driver sent a message and gave us the location where he was parked. We had medical professionals at his location within 10 minutes, and we were told that had he not [received help] in the amount of time that he did, he would have bled to death."[39]

Executive Vice President and Chief Information Officer Bob Synowicki said the company uses the system in many more capacities than most of its competitors. "I think we use it more than any other trucking company and for many, many different uses," he said. "We track engine diagnostics, and they're sent to our maintenance department on an exception basis. So we know if an engine is not performing or if the alternator is losing charge before the driver even knows. So we use it from a maintenance standpoint."[40]

Synowicki said the company is experimenting with other uses.

There are just a million things you can do with that device. One initiative would be to send weather forecasts automatically to the trucks and actually reroute a truck going into an area where a road is closed due to weather problems.

We're also starting to get information now about construction zones. If there are tremendous delays, we want to be able to automatically send information to the trucks that are going to be affected by that. It is getting so we almost talk to the driver through this device.[41]

The communication that is so vital to Werner's efficiency also works to make the driver's life on the road safer and more manageable. This added benefit to the driver acts as a selling point, drawing more top-notch drivers into the Werner family.

The advantage provided by the Qualcomm system also proved invaluable in attracting and serving dedicated-service clientele. Early recognition of this benefit justified the cost of developing the satellite system further. "It was a large investment, but we realized that to be a leader, we had to invest a substantial amount in the computer system, software, and computer-related technology," Curt Werner said. "By investing today, we can capitalize on opportunities tomorrow."[42]

Werner had no doubt at the time that the industry would continue to consolidate and that customers would seek to reduce the number of carriers they worked with. "Smaller carriers are leaving the market, which means an opportunity for us to develop more core carrier relationships. We'll be one of the major beneficiaries of the consolidation trend," Curt said.[43]

By the Book

From his earliest days as a driver, C. L. was aware of the role safety played in the trucking business. In a one-man, one-truck company, one accident could spell the end of the business. Therefore, risk minimization became a top priority.

C. L. explained, "Back then, we were a small company taking those risks, but fortunately we managed to have enough safety programs in place to keep us from getting in trouble. There were a few times when trucks were torn up.... You worry about it every night, because if I had three accidents in one night, I [was] out of business."[44]

Although not alone in its regard for safety, Werner was sometimes swimming against the tide of its industry. In 1995, the *Baltimore Sun* ran a series of investigative articles about safety in the trucking industry.

Truck drivers routinely break the law by driving their rigs longer than 10 hours at a stretch and then falsifying their logs to cover it up, said drivers interviewed yesterday at Trucker's Inn, the massive truck stop off Interstate 95 in Jessup [Maryland].

Some drivers decide for themselves to exceed the 10-hour limit, truckers said, but others are pressured by their employers to drive longer than federal law allows.

"There are companies who will require their guys to deliver a load in less time than they can legally do it," said Michael Archibald, a 45-year-old from New Mexico. "If a driver complains about it, which he has the right to do, he'll find himself not getting loads. What are you going to do, run with the load or bitch?"

Mr. Archibald has driven six years for Werner Enterprises, a large trucking company based in Omaha, NE. He said Werner operates "by the book."[45]

C. L. was, in fact, outspoken on the subject of running over hours. Jim Hebe (formerly of Kenworth and then president of Freightliner) remembered one conversation in which C. L. spoke his mind to trucking industry peers and pals alike, much to his associates' dismay.

I remember we were on a fishing trip, and the topic of hours of service came up. Everybody was hell bent on breaking into the hours of service and getting more hours. I remember C. L. said, "How many of you boys have ever driven a truck?" A couple of them had driven trucks, but it had never been their real livelihood. They ran trucking companies, but they never really drove a truck for a living.

[C. L.] said, "I'm going to tell you boys something. You start digging into that hours of service, you're opening a can of worms, and I'm going to tell you why. We don't want these guys

driving any more hours. I've driven a truck, and I know what's going on out there. I'm telling you something. If I were driving a truck, I wouldn't want to be driving any more hours. It's not safe. Making these guys drive more hours isn't safe, and I'm not going to support you boys on it because it's wrong."[46]

Building the Best Safety Program

With the safety mind-set permeating the company, a formal program had always been in place. But like all the aspects of Werner Enterprises, as the company grew, the individual departments accelerated simultaneously. C. L. not only wanted a great safety program; he wanted one that would set an example for the rest of the industry. He entrusted the department to fellow Petersburg native and longtime associate Duane Henn.

According to Henn, safety's predominance emanated from the top. "As the individual who is directly responsible for the safety programs, I have been very fortunate in that C. L. Werner and the Werner family have always been very committed to safety," he said.[47]

Curt Werner had worked closely with Henn in developing the program. "C. L. has always emphasized safety, and he transmitted that down to us boys," Curt said. It was his older brother Gary who directly introduced Curt to the safety department. "My brother Gary said, 'Curt, it would be very important for you to go into safety. We have some issues I would like you to work on there.' Of course," Curt remembered, "that's where Gary had been involved when he came up through the company."[48]

This family commitment, Henn said, has resulted in an exemplary program. "They have provided me and my staff all the resources available to the transportation industry to allow us to develop and provide to our drivers a premier safety-training program," he said.[49]

Curt Werner and Henn said Werner Enterprises was the first company to formalize ongoing safety meetings and make them mandatory for drivers. "It [is] required for our drivers to attend quarterly safety meetings," Henn said. "We provide drivers with varying subjects" that relate to the safe operation of their vehicles. The subjects cover seasonal issues, federal regulations, and other matters.[50]

Curt Werner added, "Maybe we'll have a film. Maybe we'll just have open discussions. . . . We set some programs up in the 1980s that I'm happy to see are continuing. I think if you talk to our drivers, they'll say the same thing. Werner doesn't pay safety lip service. They really believe in it."[51]

A truck giveaway was one of the more creative elements Henn and Curt Werner incorporated into the program. Curt recalled, "We bought some new S10 trucks. We had drawings for drivers who had no accidents—had no service issues whatsoever for the whole year. We put their names in a hat, and we would draw, and we would actually give an S10 pickup to the driver."[52]

Pickup trucks aside, Henn reiterated the connection between successful driver recruiting and a first-rate training program. "I believe the reputation of the company and our safety training programs have been instrumental in many entry-level drivers' seeking to gain employment with Werner," he said.[53]

The 1996 annual report celebrated 40 years of business for Werner Enterprises. This is the report's cover, by artist Mark Chickinelli.

CHAPTER 8

INFORMATION HIGHWAY
1993–1998

To be recognized as the premier provider of truckload transportation services.
—Werner Enterprises vision statement, 1994

THE TECHNOLOGY AND COMmunication revolution of the early 1990s had a profound effect on the American economy. With a supercharged stock market fueled by a boom in Internet and high-tech offerings, many Americans were awash in prosperity. Larger homes, luxury cars, and big-screen televisions became the status symbols of the new economy. It was an era of seemingly limitless wealth and excess indulgences.

Werner Enterprises would not be left behind. The company increasingly utilized information technologies to boost efficiency. By 1998, it would be leading the pack in trucking.

By 1994 Werner Enterprises had developed the tools to provide complete transportation services to its customers. The company's fleet of 4,000 trucks pulled trailers ranging from 27 to 57 feet, including vans and soft-side trailers with roll-up or swing rear doors. Werner offered vans, flatbed, regional short haul, temperature controlled, and dedicated services.

However, with growth came signs the company was becoming too departmentalized. A 1994 *Enterpriser* addressed the company's need to "reestablish a sense of cooperation and oneness of purpose." Werner sharpened its focus on training and education and created an executive steering committee to head a Total Quality Management program. One executive represented each department in monthly meetings. The program offered a structured approach to identifying, analyzing, and solving business problems while keeping the focus on the customer. "In the last five years, customer buying habits, as they apply to transportation, [have been] changing rapidly," the article noted. "Customers are beginning to put less emphasis on price and more emphasis on value. They are expecting more and better services."[1]

Other conditions fueled Werner's drive to improve operations. As the United Nations' trade embargo against Iraq entered its fourth year, diesel fuel prices increased by 10 to 15 percent. These price hikes, coupled with a dip in truck demand, slowed Werner's growth slightly in 1995.[2]

"It was a trying year for the transportation industry, but Werner Enterprises did a lot better than many of its competitors," wrote C. L. Werner in the 1995 annual report. Annual profits dipped to slightly less than $36.4 million, down less than 1 percent from 1994. "It has been a struggle to put equipment to work for truck companies, and overcapacity problems and higher fuel prices stifled earnings." Werner responded by lowering administration costs and slowing hiring.[3]

Truck overcapacity and high diesel fuel prices made for some slow going in 1994 and 1995.

Despite the tough period, the team began construction of its Phoenix, Arizona, terminal and opened a museum at Werner headquarters. Some of the first vehicles displayed were a replica of C. L.'s 1956 Ford truck and his 1985 Peterbilt show truck. The company also expanded its fleet that year to 4,350 tractors and 11,060 trailers.

While the truck overcapacity problem subsided in 1996 and freight demand improved, diesel fuel prices jumped another 14 percent. The steps Werner had taken to improve operations and tighten its belt would prove crucial to the company's future.[4]

Taking on Technology

In 1993, C. L. sent Greg Werner in a new direction—Management Information Systems (MIS). "He just called me in one day and said, 'This is yours,' and I couldn't even turn the computer on," Greg recalled. "I said, 'I don't know what good I'm going to be here.'"[5]

Greg hired Vince Robertson, his sister's father-in-law, as a consultant. "He came in, looked at all our systems, and gave me some guidance," Greg said. "Robertson got us to start networking our computers. He gave me a lot of great insight."[6]

From there, Greg immersed himself into computers, learning databases, operating systems, and even programming.

Before Greg started in MIS, Gary Werner had been very involved in the company's computer infrastructure. "Gary got us out of the pen and paper stage and into our first computers—the Quantel system," Greg said.[7]

Gary had also started a practice of developing custom software. "We had bought a canned program for the first computer in dispatch, but we decided we wanted software that was written with Werner Enterprises in mind," Gary said.[8]

Greg's move into MIS was not entirely a surprise. "Greg had run all our maintenance for a long time, and he was ready to do something else," Gary said. "We had some good people in maintenance who took over for him so he could make this move. Greg was excited. He really stepped forward. When Greg gets involved in something, it's 100 percent. He's made huge strides in our technology area."[9]

Opti Connect

Jim Belter, senior director of technical support, recalled that Greg had his hands full. "After

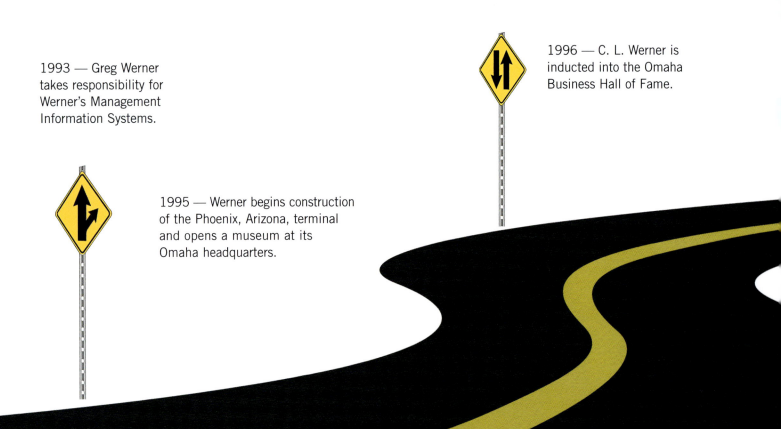

1993 — Greg Werner takes responsibility for Werner's Management Information Systems.

1995 — Werner begins construction of the Phoenix, Arizona, terminal and opens a museum at its Omaha headquarters.

1996 — C. L. Werner is inducted into the Omaha Business Hall of Fame.

the boom of the Internet, Werner pretty much had a storefront open 24 hours a day, seven days a week," Belter said. "We needed to have our systems up and available for our clients. Not only do we haul a commodity for them; we need to provide them with information on those hauls."[10]

Werner was growing almost as fast as the information from new clients came in. "We came to kind of a crossroads technologywise because we had reached the limit with the computer platform that we were using at that time," Belter said. "There was no other high-end step for us to leap to. We had slowed down the growth of the company because the technology wasn't available to keep pace with our growth. C. L. pretty much told Greg, 'You're not going to slow down the growth of the company because of some computer.'"[11]

While Greg was a novice to computers, he understood horsepower. "He loves cars and trucks with lots of power, so taking it from that approach, he embraced the technology," Belter said. "Today, he can talk with the best of them about computers."[12]

Werner began working with IBM on Opti Connect, a system that allowed Werner to link computer systems to generate more horsepower. IBM consultant Steve Finnes helped develop Opti Connect. "We linked Werner's AS400 computers together in a network at the bus level, enabling them to split the workload off and adding more capacity to the system," Finnes said.

At that time, we were in a transition. We hadn't yet introduced to the marketplace our 64-bit architecture. So there were a number of customers really pushing the high end of the product line from a processing power perspective and a capacity perspective, and Werner Enterprises was one of those. We had developed a methodology whereby we were able to create a cluster type architecture—where you were able to separate the application from the database. Thereby, you were able to split workloads across more than one machine, and Werner Enterprises was one of the first adapters of that technology.[13]

Opti Connect afforded Werner sufficient capacity to continue to grow as a company. "It was definitely a breakthrough because it enabled the AS400 customers to do very low latency, high bandwidth

1997 — New terminals are added in Allentown, Pennsylvania, and Indianapolis, Indiana.

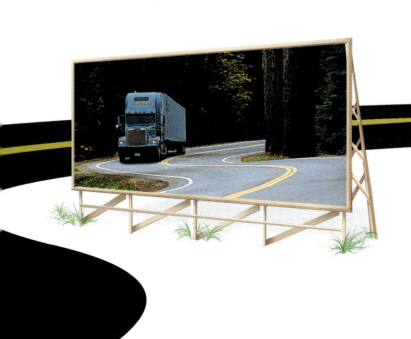

1998 — The FHWA approves Werner's paperless log system pilot program.

"Guardian Angel"

C. L. WERNER NEVER FORGOT HIS roots. But just remembering where he came from was not enough; he had to express his gratitude toward his hometown.

In 1993 Clarence was in Petersburg, Nebraska—still home to his parents, Hugo and Louise Werner, and his sister Lois Werner Bennett. He visited St. John's religious education center, where his parents and sister had recently helped pay for some long needed repairs to the convent.[1]

"In August of 1993 [C. L.] Werner came to town for a visit and dropped by to see what we'd done to renovate the convent," said Sister Patricia "Pat" Throener, principal of St. John's Elementary School and one of the two remaining nuns living in the convent, which once housed as many as 15 sisters. "I gave him a tour and then invited him into the kitchen for a cup of coffee."[2]

Sister Pat told C. L. of a plan to abandon the structurally unsound old schoolhouse and move the school into four rooms that had been added to the back of the convent. "How would you feel if I offered to build a new school with a senior and community center?" Clarence asked, sipping his coffee. After she caught her breath, Sister Pat responded, "I think I need to call Father Connealy and get him over here." The Rev. Jerry Connealy was pastor of St. John the Baptist Catholic Church.[3]

No time was wasted, and by October 1993 a building committee was formed, and architect John Armknecht of Omaha was retained. A drive began for an endowment fund to assure perpetual maintenance for the center. The old parish hall was razed, and in May 1994 construction began on the multifunctional center. C. L. picked up the $1.3 million tab.[4]

Before the center was dedicated, on April 30, 1995, Sister Pat said, "In my talk at the Sunday dedication, I'm going to tell Mr. Werner, 'You are our guardian angel.' I am also going to present him with two mementos of his old school—two

C. L. Werner donated $1.3 million for the construction of a new school, senior and community center in his hometown.

guardian angel pictures. I just think it's wonderful for someone to put this much back into his community."[5]

Bernie Cunningham, chairman of the town's award-winning Community Improvement Committee and operator of the Cunningham Cafe in Petersburg, described the new center as "a monument to the cooperative and neighborly spirit of the community. We know of no other community combining a Catholic school, senior and community centers."[6]

"Guardian Angel" C. L.'s magnanimous actions did not go unnoticed. On October 10, 1995, he was presented with the Archdiocese of Omaha Distinguished Benefactor Award. Archbishop Elden Curtis praised Werner at the ceremony, saying, "What it means to be human, what it means to be loved by God, and to be with God for all eternity, that is their destiny. Nothing else counts."[7]

connectivity between servers, allowing workload to be broken into parts," Finnes said. "Instead of executing an application and the database on the same system, we were able to separate them so that the database could be serving more than one application server, and this therefore created greater capacity. This was rather challenging to execute. Werner was one of the first adapters. They actually helped us work out the kinks when it first came out. So they were key in helping us develop that technology."[14]

Belter said the Opti Connect system has been a boon to Werner's MIS.

Greg loves options. He doesn't want to be stuck going down a one-way road. He likes to be able to turn on a dime or switch gears. So having these multiple systems is important to him. We've got three systems that are running this Opti Connect system today. If one were to fail, we can fall back on the other two. It creates a sense of security. We can't afford to tell a customer, "Sorry, our computers are down today." I've got to be able to have that information at my fingertips.[15]

Decades of Dedication

In 1996, C. L. turned 59, and his company turned 40. Werner Enterprises earned more than $40 million, more than any other publicly traded truckload carrier that year. Revenues grew 12 percent, from $576 million to $643 million.

While the CEO and chairman had no plans to retire, he continued to loosen the reins on his enterprise. "Full time used to mean 80 hours a week," he told the *Omaha World-Herald*. "Now it means 35 to 40."[16]

Greg Werner was promoted to executive vice president, and Curt Werner was promoted to vice chairman of corporate development. Bob Synowicki became executive vice president and took on the added responsibility of chief operating officer. John Steele, also a vice president, moved up to chief financial officer and treasurer of the company. Richard Reiser, who joined the company in 1993, was named executive vice president and general counsel. Jim Johnson, who joined in 1991, was promoted to corporate secretary and controller.

Accolades and Accomplishments

Werner made news in 1994 and 1995 as the only truckload transportation company to be named in two *Computer World* magazine lists: "The Best Places to Work in Information Systems" and "Top 100 Companies Utilizing Information Technology." In 1996 C. L. was inducted into the Omaha Business Hall of Fame.[17]

The company gained more recognition when it turned one of its 53-foot trailers into a mobile billboard as part of a U.S. Department of Transportation (DOT) campaign called "No-Zone." The effort encouraged motorists to adopt safe driving practices as they shared the road with trucks, stressing the importance of steering clear of truckers' blind spots.[18]

But Werner's dedication to safety was not unusual, for it often set precedents that competitors followed. In 1996, 84 Werner drivers each achieved 1 million accident-free miles, and five drivers achieved 2 million each. That same year, 1,228 truckers drove for Werner the entire year with no preventable accidents or incidents and delivered 100 percent of their shipments on time.[19]

Worst-Case Scenario

In October 1997, Werner Enterprises broke ground on a 66,000-square-foot disaster recovery site on 10 acres of land in Omaha, Nebraska. Though the company had always had a disaster recovery plan in place, the time had come to build a facility large enough to handle all the operations of the multi-million-dollar enterprise in the event of a natural disaster.

In an October 10, 1997, interview with the *Omaha World-Herald*, Chief Information Officer Bob Synowicki said the facility was designed to keep the company's trucks and operations rolling in the event that Werner headquarters was damaged by fire, tornado, or any other disaster.

"If there was something like a fire or chemical spill on the highway [adjacent to Werner's offices], and the company couldn't function at its headquarters, we could transfer most of the business to the disaster recovery site and continue operating," Synowicki said.[20]

In the interim, Synowicki said the building, a precast concrete structure with 30-foot ceilings, would be used to store records and house some computers and staff to augment headquarters operations. "If the headquarters were damaged, the stored items would be moved out, and the building would be used as offices. It will have enough lighting, heating, and air conditioning for people to work there."[21]

The location of the facility was perhaps the most critical consideration, Synowicki added. "We needed a site of a certain size and distance from our headquarters. It had to be far enough away from any problem affecting our headquarters, but close enough to be easily accessible."[22]

The following spring, Werner began construction on the east side of Highway 50 to build new maintenance buildings. "We had about five acres when we first moved to this headquarters site," Synowicki said. "Now we have more than 200 acres, and we are still growing."[23]

Checking Records

One of the ongoing functions of DOT is to perform audits periodically of motor carriers to verify their record keeping. In 1996 DOT chose Werner for such an audit. Unfortunately, a chain of events marked by personal conflicts occurred that, in C. L.'s words, "got [DOT representatives] upset all the way back to Washington. When I found out about it, they were ready to give us a conditional report—and that is bad."[24]

A conditional report meant that if Werner didn't comply with certain DOT demands within three months, it would receive an unsatisfactory rating. If DOT remained unsatisfied, "We'd cease to exist," C. L. said.[25]

Werner uses a simulator to perfect the skills of its drivers, who can hone their skills on computerized hazards such as poor weather and road conditions and traffic.

CHAPTER EIGHT: INFORMATION HIGHWAY

Above: Werner employees stand outside the expansion in May 1998 with the beam that would top the building off. The three-story structure more than doubled the size of the company's Omaha headquarters.

Right: A 66,000-square-foot disaster recovery site is always at the ready at Werner Enterprises, enabling the company to continue operations in the case of a natural disaster.

DOT representatives, some of whom C. L. knew, visited him in person. "So this is how serious it is?" C. L. asked. "And why are you picking on us?"

"Well, some of your people have a bad attitude," they responded.[26]

"I knew who it was," C. L. recalled. He asked DOT for time. "Leave me alone for six months, and I'll straighten this up," he told the representatives. He had an idea.[27]

C. L. had a vision involving the use of electronic logbooks. The Qualcomm system of satellites and computers could record truckers' working hours accurately. Not only would electronic logbooks help keep fatigued drivers off the roads, but information would be more timely and paperwork virtually eliminated.[28]

"It was a classic example of how C. L. has taken technology and run with it," Chief Financial Officer John Steele said.

We felt like we were being singled out because we were a big carrier. We had a good safety record—one of the best—and for four years, we had satellite communication devices on our trucks that let us know within a few hundred yards or less where our trucks were at all times. As we were occasionally having problems with [DOT] regarding hours of service and drivers, C. L. said, "Isn't there a way we could keep drivers' hours of service using the satellite system we have? Can we do it proactively rather than reactively?"[29]

Drivers Mike and Dottie Blanche, of Arkansas, won first prize for this Calendar Contest photo, which graced the cover of the January 1996 *Enterpriser*.

Traditionally, drivers' records were compiled from written logbooks returned by the drivers, typically some 30 days after the fact. Steele explained, "You'd verify the information, maybe compare it to time-dated receipts, to determine if the driver was falsifying any information in his logbook. If that was the case, then it was a safety risk. Typically, the real bad accidents can occur when the drivers run over hours and they're sleepy."[30] It was this safety factor that most concerned DOT, but it concerned C. L. even more.

"Drivers could run whatever hours they wanted to run, and write down whatever they thought fit," said Executive Vice President and General Counsel Richard Reiser. "And companies, by and large, let them get away with that. One reason is it's hugely time consuming to catch them at it. But C. L. said, 'Look, guys, none of us wants to think that some family got killed here on the road by one of our trucks because we weren't doing the job.'"[31]

C. L.'s log idea was viewed as impractical by many Werner personnel. "The marketing people and the safety people said, 'We can't do that. There's no way we can operate,'" C. L. recalled. Their reaction led him to think, to his dismay, that perhaps some drivers *were* running over hours.[32]

C. L. made up his mind to reprogram all the computer systems. "I said, 'We're going to do this, guys. We've got to switch these trucks out. We're going to have to check them ahead of time when we load them, and we'll have to have another truck ready to take the load on if it's one that needs to move, because we're not going to run them over hours. We're going to run them right.'"[33]

Steele said C. L.'s motives involved more than satisfying DOT and maintaining a good rating. Core values were at work. "C. L. basically put the law down and said, 'Let's design a system. It's the right thing to do, not only from a business standpoint, but also from a responsibility-to-the-motoring-public standpoint.' He really felt like if we could design a system that managed drivers' hours and services proactively using the technology that is available, then we ought to do it," Steele said.[34]

With the objective clearly stated, the Werner sons helped push the project forward. Greg Werner became a key player. "Greg was very instrumental," C. L. recalled. "I mean when I said, 'We're going to do it,' my boys jumped in and said, 'This is going to happen because we made the commitment.'"[35] As expected, the rest of the Werner team quickly rallied. "That was a mandate from him ... and as a company, we took that very seriously," said Vice President of Management Information Services Lee Easton. "We developed this system."[36]

When the DOT representatives returned, they found that C. L. had remained true to his word. "Oh, I was their buddy," C. L. said. He recalled the conversation.

"We can't believe you did this," the DOT representatives said. "*We* need to do this."

"Well, it works," C. L. told them. "It's costing us money, but we're going to make it work. Just leave us alone."

CHAPTER EIGHT: INFORMATION HIGHWAY

"You're fine," they said. "Just go ahead and do it." It seemed everyone came away satisfied. "They were so good about it," C. L. said. "They came in and praised us and told everybody about it."[37]

Paperless Logs

By the end of 1997, Werner Enterprises was working with the Federal Highway Administration (FHWA) to get an automated hours-of-service system approved. "This would save Werner drivers the hassle and inconvenience of handwriting paper logbooks on a daily basis," C. L. Werner stated in the 1997 annual report. "Drivers prefer to drive rather than fill out paperwork, and we expect this system will provide us with a driver retention and recruiting advantage as 1998 progresses."[38]

Once the project was in full swing, events progressed rapidly, but not without a price. "The first year, we lost about 2.5 percent of productivity," C. L. said. "[It] cost us some money, but we were making a lot of money anyway, and then we got our systems in place and our computers programmed."[39] C. L. had faith that the system would more than pay for itself in the long run.

As CFO, Steele also had concerns, but he believed in C. L.'s long-term approach.

When we went into it, we were concerned that we might be less efficient because we knew there were probably some drivers who were driving [too many] hours and that if we regulated it better up front, we might cause our production, our miles per truck, to drop maybe 2, 3, or 5 percent.

But we found over time that by having the information up front, we made better decisions. We preplan the assignment of trucks to loads much better than we used to. In the old days, the driver would tell us, "I've got plenty of hours," and maybe he did and maybe he didn't. Now we know exactly what the driver has available. We make better decisions. We don't make dumb decisions based on inadequate information; we make good decisions based on real-time information,

A nighttime view of the Phoenix, Arizona, shop area, containing a paint shop, two safety lanes, two service bays, a wash bay, seven repair bays, locker rooms, and a parts room

DEDICATED SUCCESS

WERNER'S DEDICATED DIVISION HAS seen tremendous growth, well in excess of 20 percent a year, and there are no signs that it is slowing down. But it wasn't always this way. When Senior Vice President of Dedicated Operations Marty Nordlund joined Werner Enterprises in October 1994 as an account executive, the company's dedicated services had made little progress.

"The first two ventures Werner had were unprofitable. They really struggled to make money," Nordlund said. "C. L. had seen enough, and he was determined to make the next one profitable. It was down in Portales, New Mexico. C. L. personally went down there and oversaw the pricing structure and the implementation of it. It was Werner's first profitable dedicated fleet."

Nordlund joined the company two years later. Since that time, dedicated services have become a consistent profit center for Werner Enterprises. "When I took over the Dedicated Division, we had four or five accounts," he said. "The accounting group developed a great pricing model, and I was a good salesman."

Although Werner was known as one of the largest carriers, the company had no experience or expertise in dedicated services. So Nordlund asked C. L. or Gary to accompany him on sales calls. It worked.

"C. L. and Gary assisted us in closing many of the first deals," Nordlund said. "I could make the most profound statement in a presentation, and if C. L. would cough, every head would turn to him. They just wanted to hear what he had to say because he was so well respected in the marketplace."

Marty Nordlund

Nordlund was pleased to use the Werners as a sales aid. "Customers would do anything to spend time with C. L. And Gary, who is the most mild mannered of all the Werners, came in and gave a sense of class and credibility to our division."

When Nordlund was promoted to director in 1995, he began working with Curt, who also lent his knowledge and credibility to the division. In 1998, Nordlund was named vice president of the division and began to work closely with Greg.

"Greg was much more of what I would consider a fireball," Nordlund said. "He is very much to the point. He'd cut right to the chase with accounts—just plain told them the way it was. 'Here's what it takes to be a viable player in the marketplace. Here's all the things working against us. Here's how we can be partners.' He really brought in a sense of reality."

Nordlund said his division is successful for two reasons. "The defining difference between Werner Enterprises and the majority of our competition in Dedicated is that we have a technological advantage. We are able to manage every single hour of a truck each day, enabling greater utilization of that asset. That ultimately covers more of our fixed cost, which benefits our customer with a cheaper rate.

"In addition, the quality of the people we hire from top to bottom makes it successful. Even though I've run it for a lot of years, I can assure you it's the people working in Dedicated that make the division so successful—and not anything that I've done."[1]

and we've actually increased our miles per truck since that time through better planning.[40]

As anticipated, the paperless log system paid for itself and continues to increase efficiency and margins. "The long and the short of it is that it's now making us money," C. L. said. "We're doing relays. We can move a load of freight from New York to L.A. just as fast as we can with a team. We're putting trips together 250 miles out and back. . . . Trucks cost less, and the driver is home every night most of the time, or every other night."[41]

In the midst of this development, revenues grew 12 percent in 1998, to $863 million. For the fourth consecutive year, Werner produced more profits than any other publicly traded truckload carrier in the United States.[42] While Werner refined the paperless log system, drivers continued to utilize the old logbooks, keeping two sets of records for DOT, which closely monitored the project's progress.

Finally, when C. L. had total confidence in the electronic logs, he played the card that had long been in the back of his mind. "We went to DOT a couple of years later, and I said, 'If we're giving you the electronic records, why do you want the logs? You have the actual data. Why don't we fix it so we don't have to make out logs?'"[43]

C. L. was asked to go to Washington, D.C., to testify on behalf of paperless logs. The government was convinced. "Now we're the only carrier in the U.S. running without logs," C. L. said.[44]

Safety Director Duane Henn spelled out the system's time line in an article in *Transport Technology Today*.

By 1995 we had an operable paperless log system that we began testing with a group of drivers. In 1996 we presented and explained the system to the FHWA, and received its approval to continue using the technology, while maintaining paper logs. We made more refinements to it, and by 1997 expanded testing to 2,000 drivers, all the while using traditional logs. Meanwhile the FHWA was studying our electronic logging, which included visits to our facilities, and gave us authorization to use it in 1998. We then notified carrier enforcement officials on the federal and state levels that our drivers were on a paperless log system, which could easily be accessed by our drivers for their review.[45]

Enlisting the Troops

John Frey retired from the U.S. Marine Corps in 1995 after 23 years as a recruiter instructor. "The normal transition for me once I got out of the marines was to get a job in recruiting," Frey said. "And that was my start with Werner Enterprises in May 1995."[46]

Frey's job was to recruit qualified drivers to join the Werner team. He found it was not difficult to do, as Werner had many selling points other carriers lacked. "One of the main things that we use over our competition is the fact that we have paperless logs," Frey said.[47]

In addition, Werner has one of the best safety records in the industry. The company's equipment also catches the eye of prospective drivers. "Our equipment is top notch," Frey said. "We've got our Freightliners, Peterbilts, and we're getting back into the Kenworth market. Our trucks have all the bells and whistles—air ride suspension, cruise control, heated electric mirrors—we stress all those things to a new driver."[48]

Artwork portraying trucking characterized Werner's annual reports in the 1990s. This cover, by Mark Chickinelli, is from the 1995 annual report.

MORE THAN ITS TWO CENTS' WORTH

ACCORDING TO FORMER DRIVER C. L. Werner, one thing has not changed in trucking: "The carrier that takes care of its drivers is generally the carrier that is able to grow and be successful."[1]

Perhaps this explains some of the success Werner has experienced. The company has maintained one of the lower driver turnover rates in the trucking industry's truckload segment.

Many of the company's programs made the driver/company relationship more stable than is typical in the industry. Unlike many trucking companies, Werner offered its drivers a guaranteed time home, scheduled runs, and the option of shorter runs to stay closer to home.

The ongoing quest for good, long-term, experienced drivers stayed in the forefront of C. L.'s mind. In 1995, Werner formed a driver relations group of experienced employees to serve as a driver resource, meeting with drivers regularly to hear concerns. The group initiated and implemented change and assisted new drivers during their first six months with the company. "Drivers who leave usually do so in the first few months," C. L. said. "We began paying special attention to issues facing the new driver." Werner Enterprises also worked to sensitize nondriver employees to the unique needs and challenges drivers face.[2]

In 1997, Werner gave its drivers a 2-cents-per-mile pay

In many ways, Werner Enterprises sells itself, Frey said.

A lot of drivers out there have gone to work one day for a company, and all of a sudden that company wasn't there. With Werner, they have the assurance that they're with a financially strong company and that their job is going to be there tomorrow.[49]

Frey said many trucking companies recruit with false promises.

We know we have a very good company, and we're proud of what we have to sell. When we discuss pay scales we'll give them the no-frills. On top of that, they can add fuel efficiency bonuses, mileage bonuses, safety bonuses, and annual achievement bonuses. But we'd rather pleasantly surprise the driver when he gets his paycheck each week rather than promise him things ahead of time and leave him disappointed.[50]

Technology is another useful recruitment tool. When Frey entered the company in 1995, the recruiting department kept records on paper. If a driver's file was needed, an employee would search trailers of files or a microfiche. But Werner's MIS department worked closely with recruiting to modernize record keeping. "We have a system we call imaging," Frey said. "Now when a driver calls in or sends in an application, a computer image is taken of that application. It's always on file. The

raise, representing a 7 percent increase in pay. This was in addition to regular financial rewards for economical fuel usage, productivity, and longevity with the company. Werner also offered a tuition reimbursement program and paid driver orientation.[3]

Equipment was another plus for Werner drivers: The company provided premium, late-model equipment that was replaced every three years. Tractors had spacious air-ride cabs with additional room for comfort on the road. Captain's seats with armrests, a writing desk, tilt and telescoping steering wheels, power windows and mirrors, and extensive cabinetry were some of the perks. When drivers told Werner they preferred conventional trucks, cabover tractors were phased out. After all, C. L. said, "a driver's truck is more than a vehicle. It is a temporary home." The company also assigned drivers their own truck rather than switch them around.[4]

Technology was also on the side of the driver. Through the company's satellite computer system, Werner developed something called the home-time system. Before leaving Werner with a load, drivers could request a "home time." The computer system monitored and flagged the time remaining until the next home-time date, and the fleet manager worked with load planners to get the driver routed in the direction of his home as that date approached.[5]

Happy drivers were key to Werner's success. Having driven a truck for decades himself, C. L. and his team treated each driver with respect. "They are our front-line employees," C. L. said. "They are the critical link between our customer and the company."[6]

"We try to do a lot of things for our drivers," Gary Werner added.

Our equipment, number one, is the best in the industry. Nobody runs better equipment than we do. It's specced very well for the drivers. We've got so many different divisions now, so drivers have a lot more choices than they did 10 or 15 years ago, and that bodes well for the job. If they want to drive long haul, we've got that. If they want to be in a regional division and get home more often, they can do that. Or maybe we have a dedicated run where they can be on the same run all the time with the same customer.

We don't want to be dependent on any one customer or industry. We try to keep it as diversified as we can, and that's helped us over the years. That's what's exciting, that trucking is such an integral and large part of the economy. There are so many involved in trucking, so many people in the country who depend upon it.[7]

recruiters can simply pull it up on a computer and turn the pages on it. That saves recruiters a lot of time, makes them more efficient, and provides better service to the driver."[51]

Drivers are held in high regard at Werner. "Of course, C. L. was our first driver," Frey said. "So there's a saying here. We treat every driver just like they're C. L. We try to do everything that we can for them."[52]

An Ambidextrous Team

It was an exciting time to be at Werner Enterprises. In 1997 Gary Werner stepped down as president, and Greg replaced him. "I was ready to relinquish the day-to-day, and Greg was ready to take it," Gary said.

It was a natural transition. Greg had really gotten into the guts of the company when he took over the company's technology in 1993. So now I'm there for whatever Greg would like to have me do. If he would like to have me go on a sales call, I'll do that. I'm also involved in purchasing. I really just try and use my experience wherever Greg needs it.[53]

But the Werners never put much importance on titles. "We're really not 'title' people, but we have to have them so everyone can see who is doing what," Greg said. "For a long time, Gary was president, and all lines drew to him. But I had been vice president since 1984, so it wasn't like I just started learning the job [of president] the day my title switched."[54]

Shaking the Industry

When Werner received approval in 1998 to run entirely with paperless logs, the rest of the industry was baffled. C. L. recalled the feedback he received from his peers. "My friends in trucking would call me, saying, "DOT is telling us you got this exemption. You're running without logbooks. It is impossible to truck and do that. You can't do that."[55]

They pummeled him with specific scenarios. "'So what do you do with the driver when he's two hours from home [on a] Friday night? You're going to let that driver go home?' they'd ask me. I said, 'No, we've got that planned out ahead of time. We don't get him in that spot. We're proactive.' They'd argue, 'No, you can't truck that way.' Every single one has come in here and looked at our system and didn't change to it because you've got to change your whole system—your dispatch and everything."[56]

Werner was recognized for its efforts. As FHWA Associate Administrator George Reagle said, "You have a company that really cares about safety, and they monitor it electronically. I think we're going to see some benefits from this."[57]

The paperless log system revolutionized the way Werner did business. Behind the scenes, electronic logs gave rise to technological advancement opportunities that had been unanticipated at the program's conception. They provided Synowicki and his department a virtual information revolution.

John Frey joined the Werner team in 1995 as a driver recruiter. In August 2003 he was named vice president of safety operations and compliance.

> [The paperless log system] may seem more of an administrative, free-up-the-driver type of thing, but for us, it is very intricately involved in the dispatching of our trucks and our whole operation. We're fitting the best load with the best truck. Every day you have 3,000 to 4,000 trucks that could be loaded across all of our divisions, and you have 3,000 to 4,000 loads. There are a lot of different combinations. Geographically, you're going to be limited, but there are still a lot of different combinations. We use this technology to put the best load to the best truck, and we use the paperless log system to track the driver's hours [in] real time. When a driver has maybe seven hours left [to] drive today, we assign him a load that matches that seven hours.[58]

Beyond the science of "best load," Synowicki used the system to compile information crucial to decision making.

> My number-one purpose as chief information officer is to gather information accurately and get information to the decision makers so they can make valid decisions on a timely basis. In trucking, things change so fast. People don't realize that, but you have to be really involved in the details to be successful. As a company, we've always been that way.[59]

CHAPTER EIGHT: INFORMATION HIGHWAY

Left: Werner's paperless log system allows Executive Vice President and CIO Bob Synowicki to gather information more efficiently and accurately.

Right: Executive Vice President and General Counsel Richard Reiser touts Werner's use of technology.

According to Synowicki, the credit for this revolution in trucking goes to the Werner tradition of being a leader in industry technology. What started with C. L. was instilled in others. "The Werner family, especially Greg Werner, our president, has been very, very involved in the technology of our company," he said. "That's been great because, since [Greg] knows how important it is, he's always pushing the envelope there."[60]

The key to the system's numerous technological functions is its software, much of which has been created by Werner Enterprises. Greg Werner praised the tools that have been created internally. "We have optimization [software] tools that we purchase that actually aren't as good as ours that we've written, our own algorithms, which we do in-house," he said. "They specifically optimize *our* business, to improve *our* productivity."[61]

Synowicki said these proprietary tools allowed the company to optimize productivity while simultaneously looking at the drivers' needs.

"People are always surprised by the extent to which we use technology to be efficient," Reiser said. "Trucking is a fairly simple business, but there is a lot of complexity in doing it well and efficiently. I've always been impressed by this."[62]

Reiser wasn't the only one impressed. Werner Enterprises was honored by *Forbes* magazine in 1998 as one of America's Best Technology Users "for its leading-edge thinking and development of the paperless log."[63]

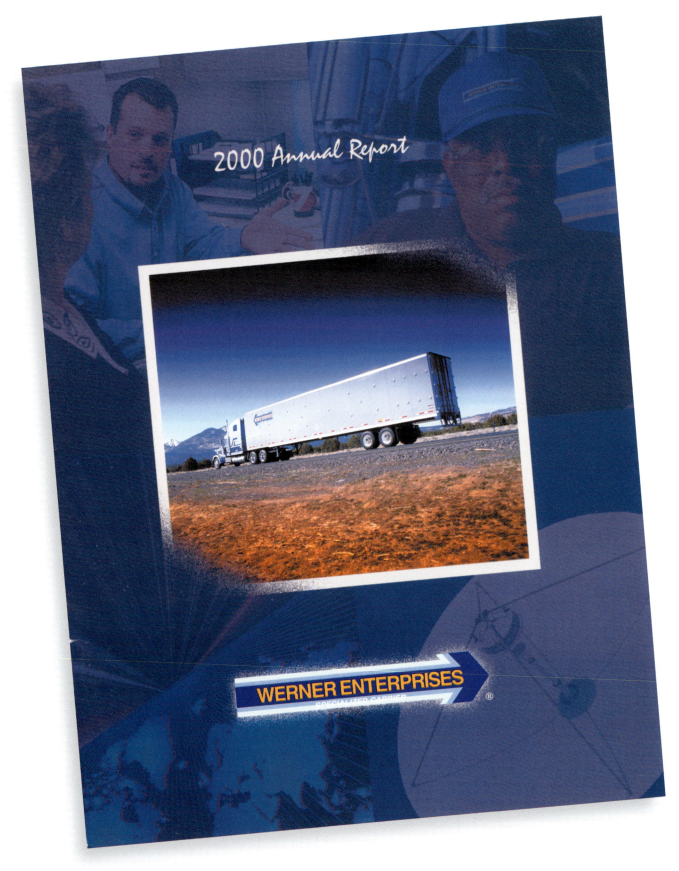

The cover of the 2000 annual report. That year Werner Enterprises had operating revenues of $1.2 billion.

CHAPTER 9

CROSSING BORDERS
1999–2001

Not only is there a very big opportunity for Werner Enterprises in Mexico; it's also been very interesting for me because of the cultural difference and the language. They're really neat people.

—Curt Werner, vice chairman, corporate development

IN 1999, AS IT REACHED THE $1 billion mark in revenue, Werner Enterprises ranked third among U.S. truckload carriers. Yet C. L. Werner didn't take much time to savor the milestone. He told the *Omaha World-Herald* he was already working toward his next goal of $2 billion. "I think the next billion will come a lot easier than the first," he said.[1]

Analysts agreed. In an industry in which large trucking firms were beginning to take a bigger piece of the pie, "Companies like Werner Enterprises have very attractive long-term growth prospects," said Anthony Gallo, an analyst formerly with Deutsche Bank Alex. Brown in Baltimore. Jeffrey Kauffman, formerly with Merrill Lynch Global Securities in New York City, said, "I think [Werner is] a good investment. It's a well-run company and is regarded as one of the leading carriers in the truckload industry with respect to service, technology, and operations."[2]

Werner, however, continued to face the same challenges that had dogged it from the beginning, only on a larger scale. The shortage of qualified drivers in particular was severe enough that CIO Bob Synowicki identified it as the "greatest limitation to Werner's growth." Still, Werner managed to do better than most trucking firms in attracting and retaining drivers. "In an industry in which annual turnover rates of 100 percent are common, Werner has a turnover rate of about 65 percent," reported the *Omaha World-Herald*.[3]

It also reported that Werner offered drivers good pay—about $40,000 a year. In addition, said Synowicki, "We give them a great truck." This included large bunks and better-than-average horsepower under the hood. "The company's blue trucks project a professional image."[4]

South of the Border

That professional image rolled onto new roads toward the end of 1999, when, through partnerships with Mexican trucking companies, Werner began offering transport south of the border.[5]

In 1994 President Bill Clinton had signed the much-anticipated North American Free Trade Agreement (NAFTA) into law, opening the borders between the United States, Canada, and Mexico. Trucking companies had always operated across these borders, but as the *Journal of Commerce*

Werner's sharp focus on driver retention and satisfaction led to a below-average turnover rate.

reported in 1992, "Truckers may haul a lion's share of freight between the United States and Mexico, but few are making money at it."

As Mike Starnes, president of M. S. Carriers, in Memphis, told a group of New York financial analysts, "They keep our trailers down there two or three weeks before we get them back, and we just hope we get them back."[6]

This environment changed drastically with the advent of NAFTA. Not only could motor carriers cross the borders more easily; American corporations could easily set up manufacturing facilities outside the United States. Werner took advantage of these opportunities. According to Gary Werner, vice chairman, "We really didn't do a lot in Mexico before that. But we've really grown our Mexico operation a lot since NAFTA. We hired a gentleman who had a lot of expertise in that area, and he has really helped us grow that business."[7]

The man Werner selected for the job was Derek Leathers, Werner's senior vice president of international operations. Leathers said it was only natural for the company to make inroads into Mexico. "Many of the same *Fortune* 500 companies that we work with in the United States have subsidiaries in Mexico," he said. "So for the most part, all the big [U.S.] players, like Colgate, Proctor and Gamble, Home Depot, and Lithonia Lighting, have some operation in Mexico."[8]

Leathers shouldered responsibility for everything from Werner's relationships with customers in Mexico and Canada to interface with carrier partners in both countries. He also oversaw the operational sales forces that represented Werner abroad. "The International Division represents the fastest-growing division in Werner Enterprises at this time," Leathers said.[9]

Werner's international operation encompassed all of Mexico; offices opened at multiple border locations as well as in the interior of the country. "Our sales and marketing force and customer service people are located across the country as well," Leathers added. "Inside Mexico we have offices in several of the major cities, like Mexico City, Querétaro, Guadalajara, and Monterrey, as well as representation offices in Torreón."[10]

Wave of the Future

Though the *Fortune* 500 customers made up a good portion of Werner's Mexican customer base, Leathers said Mexican companies generated much

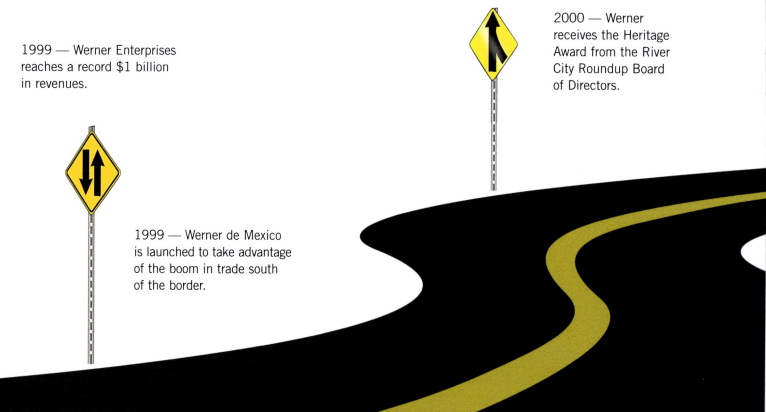

1999 — Werner Enterprises reaches a record $1 billion in revenues.

1999 — Werner de Mexico is launched to take advantage of the boom in trade south of the border.

2000 — Werner receives the Heritage Award from the River City Roundup Board of Directors.

CHAPTER NINE: CROSSING BORDERS

of the business as well. "It's a combination of both," he said. "There are many Mexican firms that now export to the United States and import the raw materials. We work with many of them, as well as many multinational firms that have operations in Mexico. It's fairly evenly split."[11]

Werner has presence in Canada also. Its operations extend from Vancouver, British Columbia, to Quebec City, Quebec. "We cover pretty much the entire country of Canada," Leathers said. There, too, Werner works with "a lot of U.S. firms that have a multinational presence, as well as many Canadian firms that are either exporting or importing [with] the United States."[12]

Leathers was most proud of the company's accomplishments in Mexico, including the launch of Werner de Mexico in June 1999. "That is the best example of the success we've experienced internationally thus far," Leathers said. "In 36 months, we

Derek Leathers, senior vice president of international operations, said the lack of micromanagement at Werner Enterprises allows its employees to do their jobs and create success for the company.

2001 — Werner opens an international terminal in Laredo, Texas.

went from doing zero loads per year to doing roughly 75,000 loads per year in Mexico."[13]

Although Werner was realistic about the unlikelihood of sustaining such a high rate of growth, it foresaw bigger numbers before things leveled off. With the incredible expansion in Mexico, Leathers felt the Canadian market had been somewhat neglected, and the company began to exert extra effort there. "We have done some business off and on in Canada over the last five to seven years," Leathers said in 2002, but the focus on Canada sharpened in March 2000. "Since that time, we've seen a tripling of our Canadian business."[14]

Below and right: Werner uses these materials to market itself across the Mexican and Canadian borders.

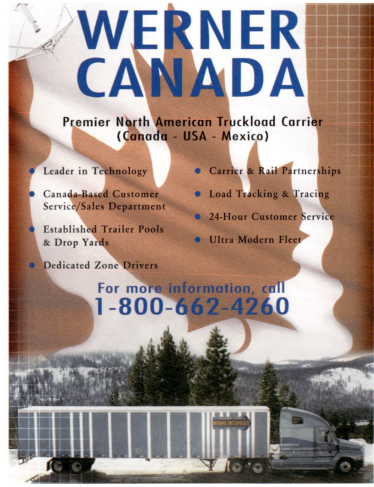

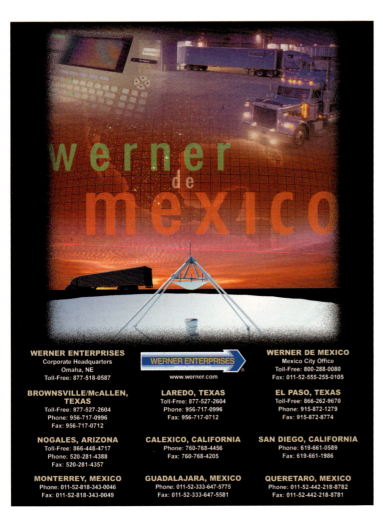

In Mexico and Canada together, Werner International handled more than 300 loads each day in 2002. Leathers called it a testament to the success of NAFTA. "It has certainly increased trade between the U.S. and Mexico and between the U.S. and Canada. Any time you have an increase in trade, you have an increase in freight opportunities, and that's been a good thing for Werner Enterprises and trucking in general. We believe NAFTA, in its original version, was a free-trade agreement, and free trade should extend to all facets of trade, including transportation."[15]

One of the keys to this mutually beneficial market, according to Leathers, stemmed from one of C. L.'s original business principles: building partnerships with Mexican carriers makes for a level playing field that is a healthier, more profitable environment for all parties. "You will primarily still see good, solid U.S. carriers like Werner Enterprises partnering with good, solid Mexican and Canadian carriers to take advantage of everybody's expertise," Leathers said, "versus somebody like Werner Enterprises trying to build a better mousetrap inside of Mexico or Canada. We believe partnerships are actually the wave of the future."[16]

This partnering has already averted many of the snags skeptics anticipated before NAFTA's ratification. Opponents of the agreement predicted unsafe, dilapidated Mexican trucks flooding the U. S. market and taking business away from first-rate carriers like Werner. But the market's idiosyncrasies kept these elements in check and ensured the prevalence of the alliance-oriented system, said Leathers.

There are multiple levels of complexities for Mexican or Canadian carriers operating in the United States, as well as U.S. carriers operating outside of our own country. . . . I think they balance the playing field. People talk about driver wages being much cheaper in Mexico and how that is a huge competitive advantage for them. Let's just say that's true. What they don't talk about is that their interest rates are almost two and a half times ours, and their original cost of equipment, due to the smaller freight size, is 10 to 15 percent higher than ours. As a result, those driver wage advantages are pretty quickly equalized by other advantages that we may have. In the end, when you really analyze it, we're on more of an even playing field than people realize.[17]

Even with incredible growth over a short period of time, Leathers still believes the international market is relatively untapped. He not only predicts continued success in Mexico and Canada but also sees the International Division opening in more distant markets. "I believe, over the next several years, you'll see Werner venturing into other potential marketplaces, like Puerto Rico."[18]

Curt Werner agreed that Mexico would become an increasingly significant part of Werner's business. "I'll predict that [by 2005], we will see Mexico become a very large, very important part of our business," he said. "I think we're going to

Werner completed a 166,500-square-foot addition to its Omaha headquarters in 1999. The 286,000-square-foot building holds a 5,000-square-foot computer center, drivers' lounges, a driver orientation section, a cafeteria, and a company store.

Bumper to Bumper

DIRECTOR OF TRACTOR MAINTENANCE Scott Reed has seen trucks rolling in and out of Werner's maintenance bay for more than 20 years. He started his career at Werner Enterprises in 1981 fueling trucks. Since then, he has seen technology bring trucking a long way.

"Back when I started in the trucking industry, we were overhauling engines at 250,000 miles," Reed said. "Now it's a million before they're ever due."

In part, what has made that possible is revolutions per minute (rpm). "The engines back in '82 ran as high as 2,100 rpm. Now they're as low as 1,450, so they are burning less fuel. Plus, we have better components, better cooling systems now."

The tractor maintenance crew oversees every part of the tractor, from the bumper to the mud flap. In 2002, the crew consisted of more than 550 employees nationwide.

In Werner's Omaha terminal, the maintenance crew can work on up to 150 trucks a day, Reed said. In its other terminals, crews work on 25 to 75 each day, performing preventive maintenance, oil changes, tire changes, and more, with an average downtime per tractor of three and a half hours. "We have a full-service body shop here in Omaha with 27 employees working around the clock," Reed said. "And in Dallas, we have roughly eight employees. They work one full-time shift."

Reed recalled when manufacturers made the switch from mechanically controlled engines to electronically controlled engines in 1988. "It was fantastic. In the [mechanical] engines, when a pan plug would flow out or there was a severe oil or coolant leak, you could have a major engine failure if the driver didn't catch it in time. Now the engine will just shut down.

"But the best, the most improved part of it, was the electronically controlled fuel," Reed added. "We went from averaging roughly five or five and a half to six and a half [miles per gallon]. It was tremendous. So you didn't mind paying a little bit more for the engine because it was going to pay [for itself]." That adds up, since drivers typically travel 10,000 miles per month, putting an average of 125,000 miles on a truck annually.

Reed expects cleaner emissions by 2007, and possibly improved fuel economy as well. And as far as cabs go, while manufacturers have come a long way with aerodynamics, the driver still controls what the truck will look like. "The truck that is preferred by the driver is the old-time flat-nose tractor with a lot of chrome," Reed said. "And the driver is the driving force of what you buy. If they won't drive it, you have to find something else for them."

Size is another consideration. "I don't know if we can get any bigger on the size of the tractors," Reed said. "We're already at 260-inch wheelbase. The cabs are 70-inch sleepers, and there will be a lot of improvements there. The drivers want more comfort. You can't blame them. They live in the truck every day. We already have double bunks, large sleepers, closets, [and] TV accessory hookups."

Reed foresees generators on trucks with separate firing units. "With the truck idling, you generate a lot more emissions than a single-cylinder generator [does]. Generators will become a requirement, I believe."

Engine idling has been a concern since the earliest days of trucking because many drivers allow the engines to idle for hours at a time. "In the old days, it was about the engine," Reed explained. "The drivers left it running because it was easier on the engine—it was harder for those engines to restart all the time. Oils weren't as good back then. Today's oils are much better. . . . Today it's mostly about comfort. Drivers want that cab to be nice and cold in the summer and nice and warm in the winter. You can't blame them. Until we come up with a solution that will create its own heat and AC without running the engine, we're going to have to deal with that."[1]

continue to see United States manufacturing set up shop in Mexico. So when you set up manufacturing, you have to ship some raw products in, and you're going to get finished product back out to the States. That's only going to continue to increase traffic coming to and from the borders."[19]

Smart Logistics

Werner Enterprises was never a company to keep its expertise to itself. It spread its expertise in yet another way when it began to hire itself out as a third-party logistics provider, working closely with customers to help them improve efficiency.

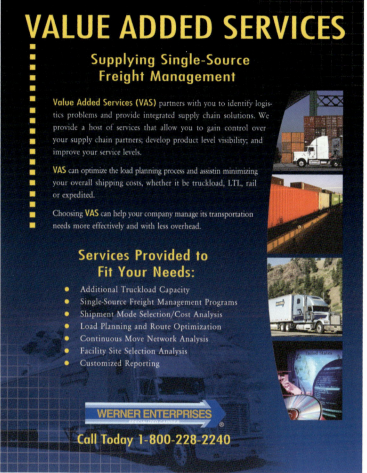

Right: Marketing material for Werner's Value Added Services. Werner helps companies streamline and improve their freight management.

Below: Larry Williams, vice president of Value Added Services, said Werner uses its tools and experience to assist customers with logistics.

"Logistics is all about becoming an integral part of the customer's shipping supply chain," said Larry Williams, vice president of Value Added Services. "We manage the process from manufacturer to distributor or from vendor to the end customer. There are a lot of parts of the supply chain that need to be managed, and we have the tools and experience to do it."[20]

The company basically inserts a Werner representative into the contracting company to assist them with things such as managing outbound or inbound loads or customer care—with Werner equipment or a combination of outside equipment that meets Werner's standards. "We have a stable of carriers that are approved to back up Werner in these special projects," Williams said.

It's a single point of contact. The customer has one person to deal with who does all the legwork and provides all the information. That person also reports

to the customer what really is going on within their business, how much it costs them in terms of transportation, cost per unit, or cost per pound, and how their transportation impacts their business.[21]

Werner has developed a state-of-the-art system in logistics management and receives exceptional response from customers. "We're here to enhance the mother ship, the asseted side, in any way we can. Our goal is to try to load the blue trucks first but, at the same time, satisfy the customer requirement," said Williams.[22]

Left: Visitors to Werner's headquarters are greeted by an impressive sight in the lobby atrium: the *Running Horses* sculpture.

Below: An aerial view of Werner's Omaha campus, consisting of offices and maintenance and repair facilities, including a parts warehouse, paint booth, safety lanes, wash bays, and body shops. Of its 210 acres, 153 are being held for future expansion.

Maintaining Maintenance

Dwayne Haug, vice president of maintenance, was in place when Greg Werner made the leap to technology. Today, Werner maintenance is one of the largest and most complex maintenance operations in the country.

When Haug started in 1990, he was overwhelmed. "The first time I sat down with Greg, he told me Werner had 52,000 wheel positions [tires] on the ground at any one time," Haug said. "I went, 'That's a lot of tires.' Today we have over 250,000 wheel positions touching the ground at any one time."[23]

Keeping track of more than 8,000 tractors and over 20,000 trailers is no easy feat, but Werner sticks to the basics. "Werner Enterprises has never strayed from the simple basics of the business," Haug said. "As long as you stick to the basics, the rest is just numbers. We have the technology to manage those numbers. But we didn't have those systems until Greg left Gra-Gar and took over MIS. That was one of our quantum leaps."[24]

As the number of tires on the road multiplied, maintenance saw several changes. "We used to have engine overhauls at 250,000 miles," Haug said. "Now the trucks run up to a million miles. We are able to stretch out the lifetime and the reliability of our equipment. So our production comes right along with it."[25]

Of course, the company's preventive maintenance in the safety lanes keeps the equipment in prime condition. "We probably run about 18,000 units through our safety lanes on a monthly basis," Haug said. "So we see the entire fleet about two and a half times in a 30-day period. We get the rigs in, checked, and improved at regular junctures. We give it a complete DOT safety inspection and tag it for any items that may need repair at that time beyond the regularly scheduled maintenance. We do that inspection in about six or seven minutes and then it's back out the door."[26]

The newest engines have fault detection computer systems. "It's been a tremendous advantage," Haug said. "Through our Qualcomm system, we can monitor any critical items on our trucks. If their water temperature is going up to a critical level, or if oil pressure is going down to a critical level, we receive a warning by Qualcomm. We've actually

Greg Werner turned the maintenance reins over to Dwayne Haug, vice president of maintenance, in 1993. Haug's team maintains more than 8,000 tractors and 20,000 trailers as they travel across the country.

sent messages back to the driver to 'Shut the truck off. Your oil pressure is too low,' or 'Your water temperature is too high.' So we've actually watched the gauges for them."[27]

Werner maintenance is a strategic arm of Werner Enterprises, sharing a common goal to deliver freight on time and in a safe manner, Haug added. "We are a support arm. We are not a profit center. We're a cost item for this company. So our goal is to maintain reliable equipment so that we can accomplish our purpose at the lowest cost per mile and to do it the most effectively."[28]

Talent in Operation

While they may not have their feet on the gas pedals, behind the scenes are people keeping the trucks rolling. Guy Welton, vice president of

operations, said while Werner is only as good as its drivers, a trucking company needs qualified people to oversee the drivers. That is where the fleet managers come in.

Fleet managers, or dispatchers, give drivers their daily instructions, and each is responsible for approximately 65 drivers. "That's a lot of responsibility," Welton said. "With that many people reporting to you, plus the investment in those tractors and trailers, they are responsible for at least $6 million of company assets. So you don't put just anybody in a dispatch seat."[29]

Fleet managers track the number of miles each truck runs every month. "Werner prides itself on being one of the most productive truckload

Left: Guy Welton, vice president of operations, said fleet managers play a crucial role in Werner Enterprises as each one is responsible for at least 50 drivers.

Below: In 2001, Werner Enterprises opened this international terminal in Laredo, Texas, despite a difficult year.

carriers out there, and that means running the most miles," Welton said. "From an operations standpoint miles are very important, but safety is number one."

To keep drivers productive, fleet managers identify what individual drivers' needs are, what they're good at, what they need improvement on, and how to help them improve. They make sure customers' needs are met as well.

"We have to make sure drivers are picking up the freight on time and delivering it on time," Welton said. "And every customer is unique. They have special requirements, and we have to make sure the drivers are informed of those special requirements."[30]

A Unique Culture

As the International Division expanded its presence throughout North America, Leathers credited its far-reaching success to Werner's conservative approach. "Our success has happened internationally as quickly as it has because Werner is a large company that hasn't forgotten how to behave as a small company with an entrepreneurial spirit."[31]

Like so many other members of the Werner team, Leathers saw the benefit of having a leader who started as a driver. "The environment and culture created by C. L. and by the Werner family is very, very unique. It allows us to make things like the international success story possible. It allows us to do what we do and create that success."[32]

The culture affects every department. While the Werners have oversight, they allow their team to make decisions and follow through, said Jim Johnson, Werner's vice president, secretary, and controller.

All the Werners give you the ability to make decisions and do what you need to do to get your job done. You can walk into anybody's office, even any of the Werners', anytime, without having to set up an appointment first. They're all open if you have a question or need something. So it is very informal.[33]

Greg Werner, who was named COO in 1999, remaining president, said he learned his management style from his father. "He's not a micromanager. He'll ask you to do something, then he's done talking. But it's more than just delegating. He's got great insight into the capabilities of people. He'll bring people in and say, 'Interview this guy. He'd be very good at this.' And he's always correct."[34]

The style has penetrated the entire workforce. "There isn't any bureaucracy," said Dan Cushman, executive vice president and chief marketing officer. "You could literally make the most monumental changes imaginable in a day, in an hour. They let you run your business."[35]

"I've never seen people work as hard as they do at Werner," Cushman added. "I think a lot of it is because not only do they work for Werner Enterprises, which they're very happy and proud to be a part of, but they're working for C. L. and Gary and Greg. Greg is here every day. People

Jim Johnson, Werner's vice president, secretary, and controller, said the company's informal environment makes for a productive and respectful company culture.

Werner Enterprises plans to follow the straight path it chose nearly 50 years ago, for it has been a successful one.

FOR THE LONG HAUL

2002 AND BEYOND

If you're looking ahead of you all the time, then you're more able to stand on your feet and keep running.

—Dick Pierson, business associate, on C. L. Werner

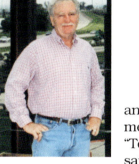

TO LOOK INTO THE FUTURE OF Werner Enterprises is to revisit C. L. Werner's formula from the very beginning: a commitment to staying ahead of the technological curve, growing at a careful rate, and attracting and retaining the most qualified employees. Werner is poised to carry on these traditions, and with them, unbridled success.

Technology

Technology has always been a key to Werner's success, said Dick Pierson, business owner and associate of C. L. Werner. "Werner Enterprises is on the leading edge of technology and doing an excellent job. It doesn't surprise me that they continue to be profitable."[1]

Since Chief Accountant Randy Dickerson started with the company in 1978, he has seen several changes in the computer systems at Werner. "Change is probably the biggest word," Dickerson said. "We're not afraid to change when we find a better way to do things."[2]

In 2002 Werner began putting together an expanded Data Warehouse project to compile and analyze information to aid in decision making.

"What this is going to enable us to do is really, really analyze a lot of different data," CIO Bob Synowicki said. "It will allow us to look at our customers and see who is the most profitable, look at each truck from a production standpoint."[3]

Synowicki said that given the market and Werner's size, information management was a mainstay of the business. "Technology keeps track of all that," he said. "We have all kinds of different technologies that we use on a day-to-day basis, and frankly, anymore, we have to use that, or we wouldn't be able to keep track of all of the trucks and trailers and customers and everything else."[4]

Dispatcher Sue Witherell, who joined Werner in 1977, marveled at the technology in place at the company. "In other companies, you'll sit back in your job and say, 'I wish we had [a certain technology] because it would make things so much easier and faster and more efficient. Someone would say, 'Fat chance of that.' But here at [Werner], it does happen. This is the most technologically advanced trucking company in the world. We have things that are just unbelievable. My family has a trucking company, and when I tell them what we're doing, they're just in awe."[5]

Most people think of trucking as an "old industry," analyst Donald Broughton said. "It has always been thought of as a very low-tech, in-rust-we-trust kind of an industry. But Werner is a

---

It has been said that C. L. Werner has forgotten more about the trucking industry than most people know about it. He has become a legend.

stunning example of how technology has infiltrated all of our economy. They're a company that has technology because it improves asset utilization. It improves the quality of life and the productivity of its workforce."[6]

When Broughton interviewed trucking companies, he often asked them which of their competitors had the best technology in the industry. "The first name off their lips is always Werner. There's a large amount of respect for Werner among its competitors."[7]

IBM consultant Steve Finnes said the first time he walked into Werner's Management Information Systems, his jaw dropped. "I was naive when I visited Werner for the first time," he said. "I really wasn't sure what they used technology for. I have visited a number of trucking companies, and I could tell you without a doubt Werner is cutting edge. They are continuously moving the technology envelope to the advantage of the entire business."[8]

Finnes was surprised to learn that Werner had hired a mathematician from Princeton University to study route optimization. "I am fascinated with what these guys use their computer infrastructure to do. They are way out in front in their industry, and I don't see a real close second."[9]

As time goes by, it only becomes more difficult for the competition to catch up, Finnes added. "Anybody [in the trucking sector] who hasn't paid attention to technology will fall further and further behind. There's an institutional evolution of the use of technology that doesn't just happen overnight. Werner is becoming more sophisticated every year that goes by. I would wager that the competition will have a heck of a time trying to get up to that level of sophistication."[10]

Werner's solid relationship with IBM kept the company abreast of technological advancements. In fact, Werner often has the first crack at testing new transportation products.

"Our IT people are chosen all the time as technology administrator of the year, hardware administrator of the year," Greg Werner said. "The awards are on our walls. We have top-notch people who love what they do."[11]

Werner has had some impressive visitors, Greg added. "I've actually had Boeing in here. I've had the U.S. Army in here looking at some of our systems and how we integrate databases, because we do some pretty amazing things. We can do stuff at a level that would scare the hell out of the competition as far as data and understanding it."[12]

2002 — C. L. Werner receives the Nebraska Entrepreneurs' Award.

2002 — Werner Enterprises initiates its Werner Data Warehouse project.

CHAPTER TEN: FOR THE LONG HAUL

A more recent example of technology at work for Werner was its mobile training centers and technology trailers. The air-conditioned trailers can be attached to a truck and hauled to different training sites or to a customer's parking lot.

"We can take the trailer right to our customer's site," Greg said of the tech trailer. "Our training trailer has the same capabilities as far as communications, but it has classrooms in it and we can train drivers in the field."[13]

The tech trailer is complete with four functional workstations, connection to Qualcomm and Werner corporate headquarters (enabling clients to track their loads), Internet access, presentation equipment, and a lounge area. The mobile classroom has the same capabilities, with 11 workstations and a drug screening facility.

Safety on Wheels

The mobile training center is just one of the tools Werner used to improve training. A Safety Management Team focused on a complete reduction of motor vehicle accidents and personal injuries using an e-trainer system that makes training available to all Werner drivers

Werner's air-conditioned tech trailer is a traveling workstation that allows customers and truck driving schools to view Werner's operations.

at every terminal. The centers are open during extended hours to fit drivers' schedules. Only one thing was missing. In 2003 Werner implemented a new training program called EDI, Educational Driving Instruction, a hands-on version of classroom teaching. The company set up courses at seven terminals and brought

2003 — Werner contributes to the Smithsonian's National Museum of American History in Washington, D.C.

These marketing materials tout Werner's "technology on wheels." The tech trailers are just another reason Werner Enterprises stands out among its peers.

groups of drivers out to the lot to give tips on backing up, tight maneuvering, managing speed and space, and making proper turns in an 80,000 pound rig.[14]

Controlled Growth

Throughout Werner's history, C. L. Werner has meticulously picked his opportunities—accelerating when appropriate and staying the course in tougher markets. Though sometimes criticized by the financial establishment for its conservative approach, time and again Werner Enterprises has outfoxed the competition through this policy of growth.

CIO Bob Synowicki said there would be plenty of opportunities around the corner. "Werner has only about 1 percent of the market share, and we're in the top five trucking companies," Synowicki said. "So it's a huge, huge market out there. I think there are like 40,000 trucking companies that have 10 trucks or more that are still out there on the road. There are still a lot of opportunities to grow."[15]

According to CFO John Steele, Werner could not be in a better place. "When things are the worst for an industry, there are certain opportunities to go ahead, and we're as well positioned as anybody for those opportunities," he said. "Our balance sheet is in great shape. Our equipment is among the newest in the industry. Our service levels are among the best in the industry. Our financials are recognized by our peers, Wall Street, and others as being among the best in the industry from both a strong cash flow and a low debt level standpoint."[16]

Steele also reaffirmed the company's cautious approach. "There are great opportunities to grow, but we have to do it in a disciplined way so that we don't grow our fleet again at the expense of margin. The margins we're seeing today are inadequate to justify adding a lot of equipment. We are trying to be very disciplined, and we hope that the rest of the industry is disciplined when it comes to pricing because cost pressures continue to exist, and if we don't price our product adequately, there's no need to add a lot of trucks. We're better off just trying to be more efficient with what we have than to add a lot of trucks at a low margin."[17]

"The Werners stress internal growth in a controlled, systematic manner," said Jim Johnson, vice president, secretary, and controller. "That's one reason, when things turn bad, we haven't struggled and suffered as much as other companies that maybe were growing faster. You almost have to hold yourself back a little bit. The Werners are very good at growing only where it makes sense, in profitable areas."[18]

Many of Werner's competitors were saddled with debt, which placed Werner at an advantage, said Donald Broughton. "Because of their debt, those competitors will be unable to fully take advantage of the economy when it does rebound."[19]

"Our debt ratio is probably the lowest it's ever been," Randy Dickerson said. "I don't think there are many truck lines out there that have the same debt ratio we have. We basically have no debt."[20]

Broughton said Werner was the most conservatively accounted trucking company in the industry. "They've been very cautious, very prudent, very conservative in how they accounted for things," he said.

They're about doing it right. The Werner management team doesn't give you half-truths. There are a number of competitors who spend a lot of time grandstanding about how great their prospects

DRIVEN BY DISCIPLINE

MANY IN THE TRUCKING INDUSTRY preach a mantra of operational excellence. But operational excellence isn't just talk at Werner Enterprises, it's a discipline of relentlessly chasing down the details and constantly benchmarking and improving upon progress already made. No matter what perspective one approaches a business from—information systems, asset utilization, insurance and safety performance, or driver training—Werner provides a standard of operational excellence for the entire trucking industry. That doesn't happen by accident. It happens because, from the top down, the management team is obsessed with doing things right and then doing them better.

Werner's management team has a long-term track record of producing strong results during good economic conditions, but that's the easy part. What really distinguishes Werner's management team is its ability to produce results during tough economic times.

In the trucking industry, fast growth during periods of strong economic growth is possible, but not necessarily wise. In fact, in 1997, the fastest-growing truckload carrier in America was Simon Transportation, yet by 2002 it was bankrupt. Producing results when the economy is faltering is the tough part. Werner was the only public truckload carrier to enter the recession of 2000 with debt and pay off that debt without a secondary offering of stock. Not only did it extinguish its outstanding debt; it generated enough cash flow to fund the purchase of a significant number of new trucks in 2002 before new EPA rules took effect. This move was seen as incredibly smart by the rest of the industry, most of which couldn't afford to buy new trucks because of their debt loads.

Throughout its public history, Werner has displayed the ability to do well in good times and bad. From its public offering in 1986 through 1999, it did not have a down earnings year. That is admirable for any company but unbelievable for a trucking company. In 2001 and 2002 Werner produced more net income than any other publicly held truckload carrier, even though some of those companies had up to twice as many trucks. Moreover, an investor in Werner could sleep at night without worrying about a negative surprise. In light of increasing concern about corporate governance and accounting integrity, it is important to note that Werner has never had a "one time" charge or restructuring. That speaks volumes. Werner's management prides itself on this history and will say, "We don't believe it's net income unless we can turn it into cash flow." By this metric, Werner management consistently produces results that outpace the rest of the industry.[1]

are, and they seem very anxious to always go out and tell the story. Almost to a fault, Werner takes the exact opposite tack. They'll let the numbers speak for themselves.

Werner doesn't spend a whole lot of time talking to Wall Street. There are times when I'm frustrated with them because they have a really good story here to tell. I tell them to get out and tell it a little. But they say, "We've got a trucking company to run."[21]

On Acquisitions

Certainly, Werner Enterprises was never quick to jump on any bandwagon. Dickerson said it was one of the differences between Werner and its competitors. "We never have been the kind of company that just wants to buy others," he said. "We've never really seen the success in that because, first of all, why buy something that you can create yourself? In today's free-market economy, what are you really buying?"[22]

Jim Johnson agreed. "We're not interested in paying two times [the] book value for a company," Johnson said. "We can grow internally with more control. If the right acquisition would come along, we'd sure look at it, but we're not going to do it just because everybody else is doing it. We've found that it just isn't usually the best thing to do what everybody else is doing."[23]

Johnson said the company has chosen its path. "I don't think we're going to change anything we're doing. I think we're going to continue going the way we are."[24]

In fact, most acquisitions in the truckload marketplace have proven to be unsuccessful, if not fatal, according to Broughton. Werner's only "acquisition" strategy comes into play when the company negotiates a dedicated contract.

"An example would be Radio Shack," Broughton said. "Werner is a carrier for Radio Shack, which had its own trucks and trailers, so Werner bought that equipment at market value to seal the deal."[25]

Broughton said some market watchers often questioned Werner on the subject of acquisitions. He recalled a meeting in which a particular mutual fund manager pressed Werner Enterprises on the topic.

They said, "Everybody else in the industry does acquisitions. You could grow so much faster if you'd do acquisitions." I could tell Bob Synowicki was getting tired of the line of questioning. He said, "Well, we did an acquisition last year." The mutual fund manager said, "Really? I missed that. What did you acquire?" He said, "We acquired 800 trucks, and we paid book value for them, and they were all brand-new. All the drivers were trained the way we like Werner drivers to be trained. The operating margin of the business was exactly the same as the operating margin of our existing business."

The other man said, "You know what I meant." And Bob came right back at him and said, "Look, you find me a business in which we can pay book value for it, brand-new tractors, and brand-new trailers, and drivers that are trained the way we want drivers to be trained, and that produces an operating margin as outstanding as our operating margin, and we'll buy that company."

It was a really good point. When you grow the company organically, you know what you're getting.[26]

The Next Generation

Business associate and Omaha truck stop owner Dean Sapp commented on another side of C. L. Werner's success. "I think C. L. is the most successful at his children," Sapp said. "He's just as successful with his children as he is in the business."[27]

C. L. glowed at his children's achievements and placed complete confidence in their continuing his legacy.

"They really learned the business, and I think that's one of the reasons that we're successful today—is that my sons do know what they're doing," C. L. said. "They paid attention, and they know what we've got to do to be in this business. They get along with people, and they've hired good people. They know they've got to treat them right, take care of them."[28]

Greg Werner said his father is a very good teacher. "I didn't take a lot of economics classes in school, and I'm glad I didn't because C. L.'s knowledge far surpasses theirs. It amazes me the companies out there that don't even understand what real

WERNER ON THE MOVE

IT'S NOT EVERY DAY THAT A COMPANY IS asked to contribute to a world-renowned museum, but Werner Enterprises will be a part of history.

In 2002, the Smithsonian's National Museum of American History in Washington, D.C., approached Werner about the upcoming *America on the Move* exhibition, for which Werner will contribute equipment and other trucking-related artifacts.

Werner's donation of a 1984 Peterbilt 359 model tractor and flatbed trailer will be incorporated in the permanent exhibition, set to open November 19, 2003. The exhibition will provide visitors with a multimedia educational experience of the role transportation played in the nation's development.

The exhibition will occupy nearly 26,000 square feet on the first floor of the museum and will feature approximately 300 objects.

Visitors will encounter the sights and sounds of transportation in the United States from 1876 to 1999. Organized chronologically, *America on the Move* will incorporate more than a dozen vignettes that showcase the museum's popular transportation collections in historic settings.

The historical vignettes include the coming of the railroad to a California town in 1876, the role of the streetcar and the automobile in creating suburbs outside of cities, and the transformation of a U.S. port with the introduction of containerized shipping in the 1960s.

As visitors travel through the large show, they also will see a Chicago Transit Authority "el" car, a 92-foot Southern Railway locomotive, and an actual piece of the famed Route 66. Multimedia technology and environments will allow visitors to see these artifacts as they once were—a vital part of the nation's transportation system and of the business, social, and cultural history of the country.[1]

Werner's 1984 Peterbilt tractor at the National Museum of American History in preparation for the exhibit *America on the Move (Photo courtesy of Richard Strauss, Smithsonian Institution)*

Three generations of Werners lead the company into the future. From left are Greg Werner, his son Clint, and C. L.

net is, how to read the balance sheets, or how to read cash flow statements to see what the real numbers are."[29]

Over the years, C. L. stood by and allowed his children to learn from their mistakes. "I let them ride some of those horses until they dropped, but they needed to learn on their own," he said. "I could have saved some money and some problems, but they wouldn't have learned anything. Now, they're making better decisions than I made, but for a while there, it was hard to watch."

Of course, C. L. drew the line at outrageously costly mistakes. "I'd let them make a mistake that costs us a few grand, but not a few million," he laughed. "Now I don't have to worry about it. I can go away for two months to Hawaii, and they won't call me unless it's something pretty serious."[30]

C. L. felt he had done well in incorporating the next generation into the business. "I succeeded there where most people failed," he said. "It's easy to build a big thing for yourself, but to turn it over to the next generation and see it go on rarely happens. You have to bring them into the business early so they learn it from the ground up. If they don't, it's a disaster."[31]

To C. L. it was a matter of fairness to the offspring. "It is a shame because you'll see a good company and some children qualified to [run] it," but the parent doesn't give them the opportunity. Then if a son, for example, suddenly inherits the company, C. L. said, "It's dropped in his lap. He doesn't have a clue. And you just sit there saying, 'Oh, I feel sorry for that kid.' He's just stumbling around out there doing everything wrong because he's trying, but he doesn't know [better] because his dad made every decision for the company."[32]

C. L. not only views his children as his greatest accomplishment but also believes they are already proving themselves. "I'm more proud of that than anything I've done," he said. "To see them taking a company from $1 billion to $2 billion. That's going to be all their deal. They'll have it there in a few years, and it will be done right."[33]

Werner director Jeff Doll strongly agreed. "I think there is no greater honor in your life than when your sons and your daughters want to get in the business with you." Coming from a family business himself, Doll was impressed with the Werner family dynamic. "You cannot believe how hard it is to work in [a family business]. But the boys do a really nice job together. They make a really great team. I think they have a great love for each other, and I think that has been passed on [from] C. L. As they say, those apples don't fall too far from the tree."[34]

Gale Wickersham, a truck and trailer franchise dealer, met C. L. Werner in 1965. He said each of the boys played an integral part in leading the company. "C. L. has taught them some good leadership. They are very well rounded. He'll leave Werner Enterprises in good hands."[35]

Rod French, a longtime associate of C. L., has also observed the Werner sons over the years. "C. L. moved each one of them around. He might put them in one position, and maybe the young man wasn't comfortable. Then he'd move him into another position. Today, every one of them absolutely excels in the position [he's] in, and they all do an excellent job."[36]

Doll said none of the Werner children was handed a position.

And if I thought they had been, as a member of the board of directors, I would have been all over C. L. about this a long time ago. But they are a great help to this company, and they are what is making this place great now. C. L. got it here, and he's still in charge. But those boys could run anything. They're tops, each one of them.

That is why I think this company is going to go on for a long time. Because they bleed blue, you know, Werner blue. They're here. And as long as they're here, I'm here. But if they ever leave, then it wouldn't be Werner Enterprises anymore.[37]

C. L.'s daughter, Gail Werner-Robertson, said Werner Enterprises has been a "university" to her two older brothers. "I think this was a university over a very long period of time," she said. "Although [Greg and Gary] didn't have formal university

Gail Werner-Robertson uses her law degree to run her company GWR Investments Inc. She said she and her brothers learned how to successfully run a business from the best teacher: their father. *(Photo by Joseph Johnston)*

training, this was an informal and very successful business model. You're not [born] with it, I don't think. You learn it through seeing it—and C. L. is a great example."[38]

Gail also felt her three brothers were prepared to assume the company. "Although C. L. really does have vision, it's often not understood that so many of those decisions are made as a group," she said. "I know the three of them talk all the time about what they see coming and what direction the firm is going. That strategic planning gets done not in a vacuum, but very much as a team."[39]

The People

When C. L. received the Entrepreneurs of Nebraska Award in 2002, Doll recalled acceptance speeches by the recipients. "They were going on about how great they were. Then C. L. walks up there and says, 'The only thing I've ever done by myself is walk up here to this podium and get this award. The rest of it has been with my employees.'"[40]

"Anyone can buy trucks if they've got the money to buy them," Gary said. "But the people are what make the company, and I think we've got the best people in the industry. Dedicated, hardworking, and proud. And that's what makes the company. We're very, very proud of our people."[41]

Wickersham said the Werners have surrounded themselves with some of the best people. "They've got excellent directors and managers, and that's what really helps," he said. "The family gets great feedback from these folks. They've got some extremely qualified people who know the ins and outs of the trucking industry. They've also got some really good customers who are loyal to them. Their [customers and employees] stay with them a long time. You rarely see turnover in the company as far as management and marketing people. You know, marketing is probably one of the most important things they have going on in the company. C. L. just has a talent for it. You've got to have the knack to do this. If you don't have the real talent and the knack for it, you're not going to be around. You're going to be gone."[42]

Guy Welton joined the company in 1987, fresh out of college with a business degree.

The recommendation is that you don't stay at your first corporation for more than five years. You try to better yourself by going to another corporation. But there are certainly no reasons whatsoever for me to leave this organization because there's just so much opportunity. The family is just awesome to work for. They take care of you in many different ways. Whether that be in growth opportunities, new positions, new responsibilities, or financial rewards.[43]

Sue Witherell said she has stayed with the company for more than 25 years because she feels she has a fair employer. "That is one of the most important things. All the Werners care about people. They're fair, open, and honest, and I think that is the reason I stayed here."[44]

Jerry Ehrlich, chairman of Wabash National Trailers in Indiana, said drivers make the difference. "I think that they attract probably some of the best drivers in the business. I've had employees all my life, and in order to get good employees and keep them, you have to treat them in a way that you would like to be treated. Werner does this."[45]

By treating employees with professionalism, Werner gained solid relationships and the best workers. "They let their people make decisions and live by those decisions," Larry Williams said. "They instill trust in us. And because of that, you would never do anything to violate that trust."[46]

Conrad Heinson, owner of Allied Oil and Supply since 1958, has known C. L. for more than 40 years and was one of Werner's earliest vendors. Heinson said C. L.'s hiring practices have brought the company great success. "His ability and foresight to hire and secure good people is very professional. I think that is where he's excelled more than all his competitors. I consider [Werner] the Wal-Mart in the trucking industry."[47]

Vice Chairman of Corporate Development Curt Werner (opposite) and President and COO Greg Werner (below) are prepared, along with their brother, Vice Chairman Gary Werner (right), to carry on their father's legacy.

85/20

When Dan Cushman was named executive vice president and chief marketing officer in 2002, one of the first things he did was knock down all the walls.

"I didn't want to see lines between divisions. I wanted everyone to work as one," Cushman said. He had an unusual way of addressing coworkers. "I began asking people, 'Can you tell me exactly what you do?' When they told me, I would often say, 'I'm not saying these things aren't important, but I'm not too sure they're things that are going to lead us to an 85 percent operating ratio and 20 percent growth. And if they're not leading us to 85/20, I guess I'd ask you to ask yourself if this is the best use of your time." Greg Werner liked the idea. "Greg said, 'You know what? Everybody needs to do that.' I started seeing '85/20' plastered on walls. It's really become our Holy Grail, our mindset," Cushman said.

Employees benefited from the 85/20 mindset. "As we continue to improve, our employees reap the benefits of it," Cushman said. "In the most difficult times, our employees are doing better. In an age when you're seeing reduction in workforces, Werner is hiring like crazy. In an age when you're seeing people getting salary and compensation cuts, ours continue to go up."[48]

Cushman said he is biased. "We've got some of the strongest sales leaders in transportation," he said. "Greg and I talk constantly about the fact that we don't have order takers. We've got highly trained, professional salespeople. There isn't any challenge these guys don't take on headfirst and absolutely deliver tremendous levels of success."

Greg Werner calls Cushman his right-hand man. C. L. calls him his last hire. "C. L. told [his sons], 'OK, I've done a good thing, and I'm done now. The rest is up to you boys to bring in the talent,'" Cushman said. "That makes me feel like a million bucks."[49]

Well, Boys:
The Board of Directors, Present and Future

The art of listening has always been one of C. L.'s strengths. He displayed this virtue vividly in meetings with the board of directors. After much discussion and debate among board members, the buck always stopped with C. L. As many board members recalled, the phrase "Well, boys" often prefaced major decisions.

Retired board member Don Rogert said there was no limit to the frankness of discussions.

Every one of us feels free to speak our mind. There's not a man on the board that's a "Yes" man. We're here because C. L. has enough faith in us to know that we're going to tell him our opinion whether he wants to hear it or not. If we're right, he listens. If we're wrong, he proves it. That's a key, and most [CEOs] don't do that. Most boards are made of people who know damn well they are to agree with everything the CEO says.[50]

"Well, boys" often prefaced brutal honesty. Sometimes it meant telling people what they didn't want to hear, said Doll.

At our annual stockholder meeting a few years ago, we knew we were struggling a little bit and that we weren't going to have a good year. All the other trucking companies were saying, "Hey, we're doing great. Everything is wonderful. We're making money. It's going to be a great year next year, so go ahead and buy our stock." C. L. stood up and said, "Well, boys, it's not going to be good. Our truck prices aren't good. Our freight is going to be down. We see that happening already. But we're going to work real hard at getting our costs under control, and we think we can pull this year out. But we're not promising anything. We're not going to stand up here and say, 'This is going to be a great year.'"

Analysts and shareholders were going, "What the hell did he say that for?" The stock price fell three or four points.

As a former Werner director, Don Rogert knows there is no such thing as a "Yes" man on the company's board. Meetings are conducted with frank honesty, he said.

Well, here's the deal. In a world with things like what goes on at Enron and the likes, you have the CEO of a company that just stood up and was brutally honest with you. And you know something? C. L. got hurt too because he owns a lot of the stock.[51]

Operating at this level of honesty was the only way to run a trucking company, said longtime friend and board member Gerald Timmerman. "You need the support of the professional business people, but I don't believe a professional business person can run a transportation company," he said. "I think this is core here. Werner hasn't lost that trucking or transportation mentality. They totally understand the business. Professional businessmen aren't running this company, transportation people are running this company."[52]

Timmerman drew an analogy to the airline industry. "I think the prime example is the airline industry after 9/11. It was probably the [hardest] time the airline industry has ever seen. Why is Southwest Airlines a success when it's costing the others millions of dollars a day to stay in business? Because Southwest is run by transportation people. Its employees are energetic, it does a good job of customer service, and its equipment is in excellent shape."[53]

Inevitably, retirement and other factors gradually changed the face of the board. "The younger people are taking over," said member Don Rogert. "Us old guys, it's time for us to move on, you know. C. L. has trained his sons very well, and they have complete knowledge of the business, which is tough for sons to do. They're trying to fill some big shoes. I think they've got this thing pretty much handled."[54]

But C. L. would not be leaving the company in a lurch. He has already selected future board members, including a school superintendent and a farmer with trucking experience. "Those are the kind of guys we want on our board," C. L. said. "We don't want someone [who] doesn't have a clue on running a business or running people telling us what to do. So we're going to keep this board, and my boys agree, we'll interview and we'll talk about it. We just want to keep realistic, commonsense people."[55]

With his sons entrenched in the company and a strong board of directors in place, C. L. is often asked how long he will play an active role in the company. Rogert claimed he had the answer. "C. L. is kind of like I am. He'll retire when they shut the lid on the box."[56]

An American Story

Werner Enterprises stands as a living example of the expression "Only in America." It embodies one man's vision and the commitment of a group of phenomenal individuals, proving Thomas Edison's insight that "Success is 1 percent inspiration and 99 percent perspiration."

But success and fortune were not C. L.'s priorities when he started so many years ago. "I always ask him, 'Did you ever imagine this? Is this what you envisioned?'" Greg Werner said. C. L.'s answer is always "'No.' He wasn't looking to grab a brass ring or trying to get to a certain level. I think it was the simple fact that he had a growing family, and he wanted to take care of them. He worked very, very hard, and one thing led to another."[57]

Greg said he respected his father because he "never lived beyond his means. He's a down-to-earth person. If he wanted to, he could have had fancy things. You'll see these companies that could do quite well, and they could weather a downturn if they had left some capital in the business, but they always pulled everything out. They had their big boats, and their big houses, and their big lifestyles, and all that. C. L. just never did that."[58]

Respect for C. L. Werner is industrywide; he is recognized as "The Man," Jeff Doll said.

C. L. Werner is the man. We have some people bigger than us, but when you talk about trucking, equipment, service, personal integrity, C. L. is the guy.

When C. L. took a load to Denver with his [show truck], he was on the radio. He about damn near stopped the traffic. Every trucker in the whole world knows C. L. is the guy. You pull into a truck stop, people would jam the whole place up because truckers want to come and meet him.[59]

A Bookend Event

BUSINESS ASSOCIATE MARK PIGOTT met the Werners in the early 1980s when he was a junior salesman at Peterbilt. Today Pigott is the chairman and CEO of PACCAR Inc., worldwide manufacturer of trucks including Kenworth and Peterbilt. PACCAR was founded in 1905 by William Pigott.

There is a long-standing friendship, both professional and personal, between the two organizations, Pigott said. "One of the real pleasures in working with C. L. is the integrity he embodies. It's always a real pleasure to work with Werner, and I've enjoyed my times with C. L. and his team. It's a class act."

Pigott said Werner Enterprises exceeds its customers' expectations with the products it delivers. "Werner and Kenworth and Peterbilt trucks have to be one of the best advertisements for quality in motion," Pigott said. "Together they set a high watermark for the industry. We have a wonderful partnership. C. L. gets a tremendous amount of well-deserved credit for structuring his company to continue to grow and provide great results. He had the vision, the guts, the determination, and the foresight to make it happen."

In July 2003, Pigott delivered C. L.'s new Kenworth truck to the Omaha headquarters. C. L. brought out his 1970 Kenworth for the occasion. "It was sort of a bookend—a celebration of the early days to the present," he said. "It was a nice reflection on a long friendship. I had a great time with C. L. and the family and the Werner team that day talking about the good days in the past, but also the good days in the future."[1]

PACCAR Chairman and CEO Mark Pigott delivers C. L. Werner's brand-new Kenworth truck.

CHAPTER TEN: FOR THE LONG HAUL

Al Adams came to Werner in the early 1980s and retired as vice president of outside terminal operations. He said the Werners are a boon to American business.

Yet with all his success, acclaim, and prestige, C. L. Werner proclaimed at the Nebraska Entrepreneurs' Award ceremony that he achieved nothing alone. His values and principles have never wavered. Timmerman testified to this character.

I've always admired his loyalty to the people who early on were instrumental. You have to have some good support people behind you, and he never forgot those people. As C. L. has gained some wealth, prestige, and so forth, [loyalty is] a quality a lot of people lose. He never ever forgot his friends or where he came from. I know his brothers and sisters. He treats them with a lot of respect. They're always included at any social function. He's always given his children opportunity [rather than] material things.

It always amazes me. C. L.'s got exceptional sensors. He was gifted. I think God gifts us all with some talents. God gave C. L. a few more sensors than a lot of other people. He gets a quick read, and he sticks to what his sensors tell him, and if they're wrong, he can turn around fast and admit he was wrong.[60]

Irv Epstein, longtime counsel to Werner Enterprises and board member in 2003, also recognized these gifts. He attended C. L.'s 40th and 50th birthday parties and recounted a conversation with C. L.'s father.

At his 40th birthday party, C. L. said he'd made his first million dollars by age 40, and he kidded about what he'd make by age 50. At his 50th birthday party, his father, who had farmed in Petersburg, Nebraska, cornered me. He said, "Irv, look what my boy did with a high school education. You know what he could have done if he went to college?" I said, "Mr. Werner, if your boy went to college, he'd be teaching high school in Petersburg, Nebraska, making $20,000 a year."[61]

The Value of Experience

C. L. Werner's business associates, friends, employees, and family agree on one thing: C. L.'s instincts paved the way for his success.

"I think [C. L.] has excellent vision and drive," Dick Pierson said. "I think he can look down a road, see where everything is at, see where they need to improve or change, and then go about doing it. That's always been the one thing that has made him so successful."[62]

"[C. L.] is a people person, and that's probably why he is successful," Randy Dickerson said. "He is really a marketer. He was the one out working with the customers—that really is his expertise. He wasn't the kind of guy to sit behind a desk and do paperwork."[63]

"Werner is a classic American success story, going from one tractor to one of the country's largest truckload carriers," Donald Broughton said. "In the past 40 years, the company has accomplished what any small business can only dream about."[64]

Even competitors praised C. L.'s success. "You really know what kind of a person someone is when you're his competitor," said Duane Acklie, owner of a private trucking company located less than 50 miles away from Werner Enterprises. "I watched him when he started his business and watched how he did everything in it. He always was a focused, dedicated person. C. L. has always had such a clear vision of where he wanted to go, and you couldn't waver him from that."[65]

Acklie added, "We're true competitors. We do the very same thing, so every day we butt heads. One day we'll take a customer from Werner, and the next day they'll take a customer from us. So there's not any more direct competitors than the two of us."[66]

However, the two harbor no bad blood. "We're concerned, but actually, if they can do it cheaper than we can, they should have the business," Acklie said. "I know [C. L.] would have the same feeling. Werner Enterprises is the best publicly held truckline in the United States. For the larger carrier, Werner is the best in the nation. I have the greatest respect for C. L. He's shrewd. He's talented. He's an aggressive businessman. But he's also very generous to education, to churches, and to charity. We're all grateful that he's in Nebraska."[67]

Investing in Good Management

Wellington Management in Philadelphia has traditionally been an investor in the trucking industry and has invested consistently in Werner Enterprises since the day Werner went public. The reason is simple, said Paul Mecray, an analyst who has worked 36 years at Wellington.

"In this industry, everybody has a tractor and a trailer," Mecray said. "Trucking companies are identical in many ways—there's no difference in physical appearance, other than something as subtle as the quality of the engine. It all boils down to management and capital."[68]

So Mecray researched Werner in a hands-on way. "I spent quite a bit of time at truck stops, talking to drivers, and buying them coffee," he said.

I told them who I worked for and asked them what it was like working for their particular company. Drivers have always been brutally honest. They'll tell you whether they work for a good company or a bad company, and often they'll tell you why. I found a more satisfied workforce in Werner than I found in other companies, and that was the first thing that made me want to go a little deeper. One of my favorite questions I asked of competitors was, "Who do you admire the most?" Almost everybody said they admired Werner the most among their competition. Those were unsolicited compliments.

If your competitors believe in you, your accounting is conservative, and your balance sheet is stated conservatively with plenty of equity and little or no debt, I can conclude you have a logical, achievable business plan.[69]

Of course, Wellington Management owns stock in other carriers too. The reason the investment company owns more of Werner is its belief that there is less risk in internal expansion than in expansion through acquisition, said Mecray. And he sees a bright future for Werner Enterprises. "I am probably their number one fan."[70]

The Legend

"There's a saying [that] if you have friends, you're the wealthiest man in town. C. L. would be the wealthiest man in town if he didn't have any money," Jeff Doll said. "There's greatness within his friends, and I think that tells a lot about a man. You look at his friends, you'll know what he's about."[71]

Doll called him a quiet, reserved man. "He's not a braggart at all," he said. "He's very kind. I'm always going to feel that C. L. has touched my life. He showed me that taking not always the most popular road, but the road with the most honesty and integrity, will get you to where you want to go."[72]

Al Adams, who retired as vice president of outside terminal operations in June 2003, said C. L. is down-to-earth. "[C. L.] doesn't flaunt that he made a lot of money, and people respect him for that," said Adams, who traveled between eight major terminals in his motor home with his wife and his dog. "It would be very hard to find a family to compare to the Werner family," which he described as "just a good family that's done a lot for American business."[73]

Jim Larsen, who retired in 1992, while his wife, Myrna, continued to run the cafeteria at Werner headquarters, said, "I can say I don't think I ever worked for a better guy in my life, the whole family for that matter."[74]

But C. L., always modest, summed up the legend of Werner simply: "It isn't like we're the smartest people in the world. We're just very persistent."[75]

Looking Ahead: Trucks, Technology, and Talent

No matter what the future holds for Werner Enterprises, one thing will remain constant—the company's focus on trucks, technology, and talent. "C. L. coined that theme years ago, and it is ongoing," Greg Werner said. "We will always focus on our talented people, our equipment, and the technology behind our equipment."[76]

But there will be change. Gary Werner said customers are concerned with the financial stability of the carriers they use. "That's a plus for us and for the strong carriers," he said. "There has been a lot of consolidation in the last 15 years, but the large carriers still have a very small piece of the total pie. So there's a lot of room there for consolidation down the road, and I think that's going to continue. It's such an exciting industry because trucking is such a huge part of the transportation industry. It is the backbone. I think there will be tremendous opportunities ahead."

"Look how far we've come since C. L. started," Gary beamed. "It's just an amazing story. It's mind-boggling that a farm kid from Nebraska could start in the 1950s with one truck and wind up here. I enjoy telling the story."[77]

Today, C. L. Werner looks back on those farm days with fondness.

I credit my success to the work I did on the farm as a child. I never made any money, but I learned. Back then, I figured it was all a waste of time. I thought I had to get out and make big things happen. But I realize the discipline alone and the work ethic was what helped me in business, because you just don't give up when you're on a farm. You stay with it. You're up all night with the sows and little pigs . . . you just do it. So once I had a business that required being up day and night, it was no problem. I was used to it. If I hadn't grown up the way I did, I probably would have been a little reluctant to do the things I needed to do to stay in business.[78]

Notes to Sources

Chapter One

1. Graeme Ewens and Michael Ellis, *The Cult of the Big Rigs* (New Jersey: Chartwell Books, 1977), 33.
2. Ibid.
3. Ibid.
4. Ibid.
5. Ibid., 34.
6. Ibid.
7. Ibid.
8. Ibid., 35.
9. Jeffrey L. Rodengen, *The Legend of Goodyear: The First Hundred Years* (Florida: Write Stuff Enterprises, 1997), 48.
10. Maurice O'Reilly, *The Goodyear Story* (New York: The Benjamin Company, 1983), 38.
11. W. D. Shilts, *The First Ten Years*, unpublished manuscript, 19.
12. Jason Cisper, *Goodyear's "Wingfoot Express" Goes the Distance*, February 2000, <www.landlinemag.com/Archives/2000/February/wingfoot_express.html> (12 December 2002).
13. Ibid.
14. Shilts, *The First Ten Years*, 19.
15. Clyde Schetter, *A History of Goodyear (The Second Ten Years)*, unpublished manuscript, 135.
16. Ewens and Ellis, *Big Rigs*, 36.
17. Ibid.
18. Ibid., 180; and Rodengen, *The Legend of Goodyear*, 35.
19. Ewens and Ellis, *Big Rigs*, 37.
20. Ibid., 35.
21. Wayne G. Broehl Jr., *Trucks, Trouble and Triumph* (New York: Prentice Hall, 1954), 25.
22. Ibid., 21.
23. Ibid., 25.
24. Ibid.
25. Ibid., 39.
26. Ibid., 41.
27. Broehl, *Trucks, Trouble and Triumph*, 54.
28. Ibid., 60–61.
29. Ralph Epstein, *The Automobile Industry: It's Economic and Commercial Development* (New York: The Arno Press, 1978), 95.
30. Albro Martin, *Railroads Triumphant* (New York: Oxford University Press, 1992) 152–154.
31. Ibid., 347–348.
32. Ewens and Ellis, *Big Rigs*, 43.
33. Broehl, *Trucks, Trouble and Triumph*, 59.
34. Ibid., 60–61.
35. Robert Leckie, *The Wars of America* (New York: Harper and Row, 1981), 708.
36. Broehl, *Trucks, Trouble and Triumph*, 91.
37. Ewens and Ellis, *Big Rigs*, 46.
38. Broehl, *Trucks, Trouble and Triumph*, 91.
39. Ibid.
40. Ibid.
41. Ibid., 92–94.
42. Ewens and Ellis, *Big Rigs*, 46–47.
43. Ibid.
44. Ibid.
45. Ibid., 48.
46. C. L. Werner, interviewed by Jeffrey L. Rodengen, recording, 28 March 2002, Write Stuff Enterprises.
47. C. L. Werner, interviewed by Jeffrey L. Rodengen, recording, 18 August 2003, Write Stuff Enterprises.
48. Ibid.
49. Ibid.
50. Ibid.
51. Ibid.
52. Ibid.

Chapter One Sidebar: The Straight Story

1. O'Reilly, *The Goodyear Story*, 40.
2. Rodengen, *The Legend of Goodyear*, 35.
3. P. W. Litchfield, *Thirty years of GY 1898-1928: A Statement to the Stockholders of the Goodyear Tire and Rubber Company*, Goodyear Archives, 155.
4. *A Wonder Book of Rubber*, The B. F. Rubber Company, 1917, 24.
5. Litchfield, *Thirty years of GY*, 157.
6. Rodengen, *The Legend of Goodyear*, 37.

7. Schetter, *A History of Goodyear,* 132.
8. Shilts, *The First Ten Years,* 40.
9. O'Reilly, *The Goodyear Story,* 44.

Chapter One Sidebar: Growing Pains

1. Albro Martin, *Railroads Triumphant* (New York: Oxford University Press, 1992), 152–154.
2. Ibid., 326–328.
3. Ibid.
4. Ibid., 329.
5. Ibid., 154, 329.
6. Ibid., 328–329.

Chapter Two

1. C. L. Werner, interview, 28 March 2002.
2. Ibid.
3. Ibid.
4. Gail Werner-Robertson, speech to River City Roundup and Omaha Chamber of Commerce, 2000.
5. C. L. Werner, interview, 28 March 2002.
6. Ibid.
7. Ibid.
8. Ibid.
9. Ibid.
10. Gary Werner, interviewed by Jeffrey L. Rodengen and Patrick LaGreca, recording, 29 March 2002, Write Stuff Enterprises.
11. C. L. Werner, interview, 28 March 2002.
12. Ibid.
13. Gail Werner-Robertson, speech.
14. C. L. Werner, interview, 28 March 2002.
15. Ibid.
16. Ibid.
17. Ibid.
18. Ibid.
19. Wayne Childers, interviewed by Richard F. Hubbard, recording, 30 August 2002, Write Stuff Enterprises.
20. Ibid.
21. Ibid.
22. Ibid.
23. Jeff Doll, interviewed by Richard F. Hubbard, recording, 29 March 2002, Write Stuff Enterprises.
24. Zeph Telpner, "The Real Genius of Clarence L. Werner Is Friendship" *The Midlands Business Journal,* 10–16 March 1989, A, 5.
25. Ibid.
26. Conrad Heinson, interviewed by Richard F. Hubbard, recording, 5 September 2002, Write Stuff Enterprises.
27. Ibid.
28. Greg Werner, interviewed by Richard F. Hubbard, recording, 16 May 2002, Write Stuff Enterprises.
29. Gerald Timmerman, interviewed by Richard F. Hubbard, recording, 29 March 2002, Write Stuff Enterprises.
30. Ibid.
31. Duane Acklie, interviewed by Richard F. Hubbard, recording, 20 August 2002, Write Stuff Enterprises.
32. Donna Johnson, interviewed by Richard F. Hubbard, recording, 16 May 2002, Write Stuff Enterprises.
33. Gail Werner-Robertson, interviewed by Richard F. Hubbard, recording, 16 May 2002, Write Stuff Enterprises.
34. Ibid
35. Ibid.
36. Gary Werner, interview.
37. Ibid.
38. Greg Werner, interview.
39. Ibid.
40. Curt Werner, interviewed by Richard F. Hubbard, recording, 15 May 2002, Write Stuff Enterprises.
41. Gail Werner-Robertson, interview.
42. Curt Werner, interview.
43. Greg Werner, interview.
44. Ibid.
45. Curt Werner, interview.

Chapter Two Sidebar: Knights of the Road

1. C. L. Werner, interview, 28 March 2002.

Chapter Three

1. Cecil Curry, interviewed by Richard F. Hubbard, recording, 22 August 2002, Write Stuff Enterprises.
2. C. L. Werner, interview, 28 March 2002.
3. Cecil Curry, interview.
4. Ibid.
5. Sharon Curry, interviewed by Richard F. Hubbard, recording, 22 August 2002, Write Stuff Enterprises.
6. Ibid.
7. Ibid.
8. Ibid.
9. Donna Johnson, interview.
10. Ibid.
11. Ibid.
12. C. L. Werner, interview, 28 March 2002.
13. Donna Johnson, interview.
14. Ibid.
15. Ibid.
16. C. L. Werner, interview, 28 March 2002.
17. Jim Larsen, interviewed by Jeffrey L. Rodengen and Patrick LaGreca, recording, 29 March 2002, Write Stuff Enterprises.
18. C. L. Werner, interview, 28 March 2002.
19. Larsen, interview.
20. Ibid.
21. Ibid.
22. Ibid.
23. John Keenan, interviewed by Richard F. Hubbard, recording, 21 August 2002, Write Stuff Enterprises.
24. Ibid.
25. Ibid.
26. Lee Hays, interviewed by Richard F. Hubbard, recording, 20 August 2002, Write Stuff Enterprises.
27. Ibid.
28. Ibid.
29. Ibid.
30. Ibid.
31. Wilbur Smith, interviewed by Richard F. Hubbard, recording, 30 August 2002, Write Stuff Enterprises.
32. J. D. Farris, interviewed by Richard F. Hubbard, recording, 8 August 2002, Write Stuff Enterprises.
33. C. L. Werner, interview, 28 March 2002.
34. Buddy Payton, interviewed by Jeffrey L. Rodengen, recording, 29 March 2002, Write Stuff Enterprises.
35. Ibid.
36. Ibid.
37. Ibid.
38. Larsen, interview.
39. Payton, interview.
40. Larsen, interview.

41. C. L. Werner interview, 28 March 2002.
42. Ibid.
43. Ibid.
44. Ibid.
45. Ibid.
46. Patricia Packett, interviewed by Richard F. Hubbard, recording, 3 September 2002, Write Stuff Enterprises.
47. Ibid.

**Chapter Three Sidebar:
C. L. and the Extra Mile**

1. C. L. Werner, interview, 28 March 2002.

Chapter Four

1. C. L. Werner, interview, 28 March 2002.
2. Larsen, interview.
3. "Werner Starts Office Building," *Midlands Business Journal*, 7 May 1976.
4. "New Business Sets Open House in Central Sarpy," *The Papillion Times*, 19 May 1977.
5. Ibid.
6. "Werner Starts Office Building."
7. C. L. Werner, interview, 28 March 2002.
8. "Trucker Selects Nebraska Site," *Sunday World-Herald Magazine of the Midlands*, 2 May 1976, C, 10.
9. "Werner Starts Office Building."
10. "New Business Sets Open House in Central Sarpy."
11. Leonard Johnson, "Drive for Success," *Sunday World–Herald Magazine of the Midlands*, 26 October 1986, 16.
12. Ibid.
13. Gail Werner-Robertson, interview.
14. C. L. Werner, interview, 28 March 2002.
15. Ibid.
16. Randy Dickerson, interviewed by Richard F. Hubbard, recording, 29 March 2002, Write Stuff Enterprises.
17. Ibid.
18. Ibid.
19. Donna Johnson, interview.
20. Payton, interview.
21. Ibid.
22. Ibid.
23. Ibid.
24. Donna Johnson, interview.
25. Ibid.
26. Payton, interview.
27. C. L. Werner, interview, 28 March 2002.
28. Gail Werner-Robertson, interview.
29. C. L. Werner, interview, 28 March 2002.
30. Ibid.
31. Donna Johnson, interview.
32. C. L. Werner, interview, 28 March 2002.
33. Greg Werner, interview.
34. Gary Werner, interview.
35. Larsen, interview.
36. Gail Werner-Robertson, interview.
37. Ibid.
38. C. L. Werner, interview, 28 March 2002.
39. Thomas Gale Moore, "Trucking Deregulation," *The Concise Encyclopedia of Economics*, <http://www.econlib.org>
40. C. L. Werner, interview, 28 March 2002.
41. Larsen, interview.
42. Ibid.
43. C. L. Werner, interview, 28 March 2002.
44. Irving Epstein, interviewed by Richard F. Hubbard, recording, 16 May 2002, Write Stuff Enterprises.
45. Dickerson, interview.
46. C. L. Werner, interview, 28 March 2002.

**Chapter Four Sidebar:
Regulations and the Leisure Suit**

1. Greg Werner, interview.

Chapter Four Sidebar: A Boss and a Friend

1. Don Bacon, interviewed by Richard F. Hubbard, recording, 28 August 2002, Write Stuff Enterprises.

Chapter Five

1. Moore, "Trucking Deregulation."
2. Ibid.
3. "Consumer Cost of Continued State Motor Carrier Regulation," House Report, 101–813, 101st Congress, 5 October 1990.
4. Johnson, "Drive for Success."
5. C. L. Werner, interview, 28 March 2002.
6. Bill Legg, interviewed by Richard F. Hubbard, recording, 21 August 2002, Write Stuff Enterprises.
7. C. L. Werner, interview, 28 March 2002.
8. Ibid.
9. Ibid.
10. Ibid.
11. Legg, interview.
12. C. L. Werner, interview, 28 March 2002.
13. Gary Werner, interview.
14. Ibid.
15. Greg Werner, interview.
16. Gary Werner, interview.
17. Ibid.
18. Ibid.
19. Ibid.
20. Ibid.
21. Ibid.
22. Scott Robertson, interviewed by Richard F. Hubbard, recording, 15 May 2002, Write Stuff Enterprises.
23. Gail Werner-Robertson, interview.
24. Robertson, interview.
25. Ibid.
26. Information provided by Richard Reiser to Heather Deeley, August 2003.
27. C. L. Werner, interview, 28 March 2002.
28. Ibid.
29. Ibid.
30. Jim Hebe, interviewed by Richard F. Hubbard, recording, 30 September 2002, Write Stuff Enterprises.
31. Ibid.
32. Ibid.
33. Ibid.
34. Ibid.
35. Ibid.
36. Rod French, interviewed by Richard F. Hubbard, recording, 27 August 2002, Write Stuff Enterprises.
37. Bob Synowicki, interviewed by Jeffrey L. Rodengen and Patrick LaGreca, recording, 29 March 2002, Write Stuff Enterprises.
38. C. L. Werner, interview, 28 March 2002.

39. Gene Hansohn, interviewed by Richard F. Hubbard, recording, 15 May 2002, Write Stuff Enterprises.
40. Ibid.
41. Ibid.
42. Johnson, "Drive for Success."

Chapter Six

1. Werner Enterprises Annual Report, 1986, 4.
2. Ibid.
3. Ibid.
4. Epstein, interview.
5. Curt Werner, interview.
6. Gary Werner, interview.
7. Greg Werner, interview.
8. Legg, interview.
9. Ibid.
10. Johnson, "Drive for Success."
11. Dickerson, interview.
12. Ibid.
13. Johnson, "Drive for Success."
14. Synowicki, interview.
15. Brian S. Moskal, "Enough Premium Carriers in the '90s? Don't Bet on It," *Industry Week*, 21 August 1989.
16. Lisa Scheer, "We Want to Be a Federal Express," *Forbes*, 12 December 1988, 71.
17. Werner Enterprises Annual Report, 1987, 2.
18. Gary Werner, interview.
19. "Werner Trucking Keeps on Growing," *Nebraska Trucker*, December 1988, 4–6.
20. Werner Enterprises Annual Report, 1988, 1.
21. Ibid.
22. Ibid.
23. Werner Enterprises Annual Report, 1987, 1.
24. "Werner Trucking Keeps on Growing."
25. Werner Enterprises Annual Report, 1988, 1.
26. Ibid.
27. Werner Enterprises Annual Report, 1989, 2.
28. Ibid.
29. Ibid.
30. John Steele, interviewed by Jeffrey L. Rodengen, recording, 29 March 2002, Write Stuff Enterprises.
31. Ibid.
32. Ibid.
33. Moskal, "Enough Premium Carriers?"
34. Ibid.
35. Werner Enterprises Annual Report, 1989, 1.

Chapter Seven

1. Werner Enterprises Annual Report, 1990, 1.
2. Ibid.
3. Werner Enterprises Annual Report, 1990, 2.
4. Joseph Mack, "Conservation: A Major Challenge for the Nineties," *The Enterpriser*, 1990, 14.
5. Brian Moskal, "It's a Year for Type A Personality in Trucking," *Industry Week*, 2 April 1990.
6. Ibid.
7. Ibid.
8. Ibid.
9. Ibid.
10. Ibid.
11. Ibid.
12. Guy Welton, interviewed by Richard F. Hubbard, recording, 4 November 2002, Write Stuff Enterprises.
13. Ibid.
14. Larry Williams, interviewed by Richard F. Hubbard, recording, 15 April 2003, Write Stuff Enterprises.
15. Mary De Zutter, "Werner Trucks Roll Into New Fields," *Sunday World-Herald Magazine of the Midlands*, 14 November 1993, M1.
16. Ibid.
17. Ibid.
18. Marty Nordlund, interviewed by Richard F. Hubbard, recording, 8 April 2003, Write Stuff Enterprises.
19. De Zutter, "Werner Trucks Roll."
20. Curt Werner, interview.
21. De Zutter, "Werner Trucks Roll."
22. Ibid.
23. Ibid.
24. Ibid.
25. Ibid.
26. Ibid.
27. Ibid.
28. Ibid.
29. Dwayne Haug, interviewed by Jeffrey L. Rodengen, recording, 7 May 2003, Write Stuff Enterprises.
30. Ibid.
31. "Qualcomm wins $12 Million Werner Pact," PR Newswire Association, 24 September 1992.
32. Dane Hamilton, "Eye in the Sky Tracks Truckers," *Journal of Commerce*, 19 October 1992, 5C.
33. Lee Easton, interviewed by Richard F. Hubbard, recording, 27 August 2002, Write Stuff Enterprises.
34. Ibid.
35. Ibid.
36. Ibid.
37. Curt Werner, interview.
38. C. L. Werner, interview, 28 March 2002.
39. Duane Henn, interviewed by Richard F. Hubbard, recording, 20 August 2002, Write Stuff Enterprises.
40. Synowicki, interview.
41. Ibid.
42. Curt Werner, interview.
43. Ibid.
44. C. L. Werner, interview, 28 March 2002.
45. Tom Keyser, "Falsification of Logs Said to Be Common," *Baltimore Sun*, 21 June 1995, 1A.
46. Hebe, interview.
47. Henn, interview.
48. Curt Werner, interview.
49. Henn, interview.
50. Ibid.
51. Curt Werner, interview.
52. Ibid.
53. Henn, interview.

Chapter Eight

1. *The Enterpriser*, 1994.
2. Matt Kelley, "Fuel Costs Give Werner Bumpy Ride in Quarter," *Omaha World-Herald*, 15 May 1996.
3. Werner Enterprises Annual Report, 1995.
4. Ibid.
5. Greg Werner, interview.
6. Ibid.
7. Ibid.
8. Gary Werner, interview.
9. Ibid.
10. Jim Belter, interviewed by Richard F. Hubbard, recording, 15 May 2003, Write Stuff Enterprises.
11. Ibid.
12. Ibid.

13. Steve Finnes, interviewed by Richard F. Hubbard, recording, 15 May 2003, Write Stuff Enterprises.
14. Ibid.
15. Belter, interview.
16. "Werner Does Safety Check on Gretna Fire Department," *Gretna Guide & News*, 3 July 1996.
17. Ibid.
18. "Another No-Zone Premiere," *Nebraska Trucker*, June 1996.
19. Werner Enterprises Annual Report, 1996.
20. Synowicki, interview.
21. Ibid.
22. Ibid.
23. Ibid.
24. C. L. Werner, interview, 28 March 2002.
25. Ibid.
26. Ibid.
27. Ibid.
28. Ibid.
29. Steele, interview.
30. Ibid.
31. Richard Reiser, interviewed by Jeffrey L. Rodengen, recording, 28 March 2002, Write Stuff Enterprises.
32. C. L. Werner, interview, 28 March 2002.
33. Ibid.
34. Steele, interview.
35. C. L. Werner, interview, 28 March 2002.
36. Easton, interview.
37. C. L. Werner, interview, 28 March 2002.
38. Werner Enterprises Annual Report, 1997.
39. C. L. Werner, interview, 28 March 2002.
40. Steele, interview.
41. C. L. Werner, interview, 28 March 2002.
42. Werner Enterprises Annual Report, 1998.
43. C. L. Werner, interview, 28 March 2002.
44. Ibid.
45. *Transport Technology Today*, 1 December 2000, 10.
46. John Frey, interviewed by Richard F. Hubbard, recording, 25 August 2003, Write Stuff Enterprises.
47. Ibid.
48. Ibid.
49. Ibid.
50. Ibid.
51. Ibid.
52. Ibid.
53. Gary Werner, interview.
54. Greg Werner, interview.
55. C. L. Werner, interview, 28 March 2002.
56. Ibid.
57. Jim Rasmussen, "Werner to Be First to Use Electric Driver Log System," *Omaha World-Herald*, 10 June 1998.
58. Synowicki, interview.
59. Ibid.
60. Ibid.
61. Greg Werner, interview.
62. Reiser, interview.
63. *Transport Technology Today*, 1 December 2000, 10.

Chapter Eight Sidebar: "Guardian Angel"

1. Tom Allan, "'Guardian Angel' Provides Blessing," *Omaha World-Herald*, 29 April 1995, 49.
2. Ibid.
3. Ibid.
4. Ibid.
5. Ibid.
6. Ibid.
7. *The Catholic Voice*, Omaha, 13 October 1995, 3.

Chapter Eight Sidebar: Dedicated Success

1. Nordlund, interview.

Chapter Eight Sidebar: More than Its Two Cents' Worth

1. Werner Enterprises Annual Report, 1995.
2. Ibid.
3. Werner Enterprises Annual Report, 1997.
4. Werner Enterprises Annual Report, 1995.
5. Werner Enterprises Annual Report, 1997.
6. Ibid.
7. Gary Werner, interview.

Chapter Nine

1. Jim Rasmussen, "Trucking Firm Gains Speed as it Nears $1 Billion Mark," *Omaha World-Herald*, 22 June 1999.
2. Ibid.
3. Ibid.
4. Synowicki, interview.
5. "Profits Elusive in Mexico," *Journal of Commerce*, 16 March 1992, 36.
6. Ibid.
7. Gary Werner, interview.
8. Derek Leathers, interviewed by Richard F. Hubbard, recording, 4 Sept. 2002, Write Stuff Enterprises.
9. Ibid.
10. Ibid.
11. Ibid.
12. Ibid.
13. Ibid.
14. Ibid.
15. Ibid.
16. Ibid.
17. Ibid.
18. Ibid.
19. Curt Werner, interview.
20. Williams, interview.
21. Ibid.
22. Ibid.
23. Haug, interview.
24. Ibid.
25. Ibid.
26. Ibid.
27. Ibid.
28. Ibid.
29. Welton, interview.
30. Ibid.
31. Leathers, interview.
32. Ibid.
33. Jim Johnson, interviewed by Richard F. Hubbard, recording, 29 March 2002, Write Stuff Enterprises.
34. Greg Werner, interview.
35. Dan Cushman, interviewed by Richard F. Hubbard, recording, 17 April 2003, Write Stuff Enterprises.
36. Ibid.
37. Belter, interview.
38. Welton, interview.
39. Gary Werner, interview.
40. Greg Werner, interview.
41. Gary Werner, interview.
42. Steele, interview.
43. Donald Broughton, interviewed by Richard F. Hubbard, recording, 30 August 2002, Write Stuff Enterprises.
44. Steele, interview.
45. Broughton, interview.
46. Ibid.

47. Ibid.
48. Steele, interview.
49. Werner Enterprises Annual Report, 2000, letter to shareholders.
50. John D. Schulz, "'Squeeze' Play," *Traffic World*, 28 February 2000, 16.
51. Ibid.
52. Henn, interview.
53. Ibid.
54. Ibid.
55. Ibid.
56. Ibid.
57. Ibid.
58. Gary Werner, interview.
59. Ibid.
60. Ibid.
61. Steele, interview.
62. Ibid.
63. Grace Shim, "Werner Dodges Difficulties," *Omaha World-Herald*, 24 January 2002, 1D; and C. L. Werner, interview, 28 March 2002.
64. Elizabeth Kelleher, "Investing: Trucking Awaits the Next Boom," *New York Times*, 9 December 2001, Section 3, 8.
65. Werner Enterprises Annual Report, 2001.
66. Ibid.
67. Shim, "Werner Dodges Difficulties;" and C. L. Werner, interview, 28 March 2002.
68. "Werner Opens Terminal in Laredo, Texas," *Trailer/Body Builders*, June 2001.
69. Werner Enterprises Annual Report, 2001.
70. Ibid.
71. Broughton, interview.
72. Werner Enterprises Annual Report, 2001.
73. Jim Johnson, interview.
74. Ibid.
75. Kelley, "Fuel Costs."

Chapter Nine Sidebar: Bumper to Bumper

1. Scott Reed, interviewed by Jeffrey L. Rodengen, recording, 28 March 2002, Write Stuff Enterprises.

Chapter Ten

1. Dick Pierson, interviewed by Richard F. Hubbard, recording, 22 August 2002, Write Stuff Enterprises.

2. Dickerson, interview.
3. Synowicki, interview.
4. Ibid.
5. Sue Witherell, interviewed by Richard F. Hubbard, recording, 16 May 2002, Write Stuff Enterprises.
6. Broughton, interview.
7. Ibid.
8. Finnes, interview.
9. Ibid.
10. Ibid.
11. Greg Werner, interview.
12. Ibid.
13. Ibid.
14. Werner Enterprises brochure, 2003.
15. Synowicki, interview.
16. Steele, interview.
17. Ibid.
18. Jim Johnson, interview.
19. Broughton, interview.
20. Dickerson, interview.
21. Broughton, interview.
22. Dickerson, interview.
23. Jim Johnson, interview.
24. Ibid.
25. Broughton, interview.
26. Ibid.
27. Dean Sapp, interviewed by Richard F. Hubbard, recording, 31 August 2002, Write Stuff Enterprises.
28. C. L. Werner, interview, 28 March 2002.
29. Greg Werner, interview.
30. C. L. Werner, interview, 28 March 2002.
31. Ibid.
32. Ibid.
33. Ibid.
34. Doll, interview.
35. Gale Wickersham, interviewed by Richard F. Hubbard, recording, 15 May 2002, Write Stuff Enterprises.
36. French, interview.
37. Doll, interview.
38. Gail Werner-Robertson, interview.
39. Ibid.
40. Doll, interview.
41. Gary Werner, interview.
42. Wickersham, interview.
43. Welton, interview.
44. Witherell, interview.
45. Jerry Ehrlich, interviewed by Richard F. Hubbard, recording, 20 August 2002, Write Stuff Enterprises.
46. Williams, interview.

47. Heinson, interview.
48. Cushman, interview.
49. Greg Werner, interview.
50. Don Rogert, interviewed by Richard F. Hubbard, recording, 29 March 2002.
51. Doll, interview.
52. Timmerman, interview.
53. Ibid.
54. Rogert, interview.
55. C. L. Werner, interview, 28 March 2002.
56. Rogert, interview.
57. Greg Werner, interview.
58. Ibid.
59. Doll, interview.
60. Timmerman, interview.
61. Epstein, interview.
62. Pierson, interview.
63. Dickerson, interview.
64. Broughton, interview.
65. Acklie, interview.
66. Ibid.
67. Ibid.
68. Paul Mecray, interviewed by Richard F. Hubbard, recording, 13 August 2003, Write Stuff Enterprises.
69. Ibid.
70. Ibid.
71. Doll, interview.
72. Ibid.
73. Al Adams, interviewed by Richard F. Hubbard, recording, 27 August 2002, Write Stuff Enterprises.
74. Larsen, interview.
75. C. L. Werner, interview, 18 August 2003.
76. Greg Werner, interview.
77. Gary Werner, interview.
78. C. L. Werner, interview, 18 August 2003.

Chapter Ten Sidebar: Driven by Discipline

1. Broughton, interview.

Chapter Ten Sidebar: Werner on the Move

1. Information provided by Lisa Fairbairn to Heather Deeley, August 2003.

Chapter Ten Sidebar: A Bookend Event

1. Mark Pigott, interviewed by Jeffrey L. Rodengen, recording, 15 August 2003, Write Stuff Enterprises.

INDEX

Page numbers in italics indicate photographs.

A

accounting, 36, 48–49, 50, 73–74, 127
Acklie, Duane, 32, 138
acquisitions, 128
Adams, Al, 137, *137,* 138–139
A.G. Edwards & Sons, 119, 120
Alex. Brown & Sons, 58, 69, 72, 75, 79
Allied Oil and Supply, 31, 133
American Trucking Association (ATA), 18, 57
America on the Move exhibition, 129
Anderson, Arthur, 69, 74
annual reports, 67–68, 72, 77, 81, *81, 90,* 91, 99, *106*
Archibald, Michael, 88
Armknecht, John, 94
Armstrong Tire, 59

A. T. Kearney, 75
authority. *See* transportation authority
awards
    America's Best Technology Users, 105
    Archdiocese of Omaha Distinguished Benefactor Award, 94
    Best Places to Work in Information Systems, 95
    Business Hall of Fame, 92
    Heritage Award, 108
    Nebraska Entrepreneurs' Award, 124, 132, 137
    Top 100 Companies Utilizing Information Technology, 95

B

Bacon, Don, 52
Baltimore Sun, 88
Belter, Jim, 92–93

Broughton, Donald, 118–119, 123–124, 127–128
Bryne, Patrick, 75
Builders Transport, 71

C

Canada operations, 108–110
Carter, Jimmy, 55, 57
certificate of public convenience and necessity, 18
Chessareck, Irv, 49
Chickinelli, Mark
    artwork, *84, 90, 101*
Childers, Wayne, 29, 30
Clincher tires, 16–17
Clinton, Bill, 107
Community Improvement Committee, 94
computers
    accounting, 48–49
    Data Warehouse project, 123
    information technology (IT), 123–124

networking, 92–93
Opti Connect, 93, 95
Quantel 1 system, 50, 92
route optimization, 124
Computer World, 95
Connealy, Jerry (Reverend), 94
core carrier concept, 71, 75, 79–80
Council Bluffs, Iowa, 31, 45
Crawford, Robert, 38
Crete Carrier Corporation, 32
Cummins, 20
Cunningham, Bernie, 94
Curry, Cecil, 35, 36, *37*
Curry, Sharon, 35–36
Curtis, Elden (Archbishop), 94
Cushman, Dan, 117, *118*, 133–134

D

Daimler Benz, 11, 12
Data Warehouse project, 123, 124
debt
    paying down, 81, 121
    ratio, 127
Dedicated Division, 78, 81–83, 100, 103
Department of Transportation (DOT), 20
    audits, 96–99, 101
    No-Zone, 95
deregulation, 43, 54–55, 57–59, 61, 69–70, 72, 78

Dickerson, Randy, 48–49, 123
disaster recovery site, 95–96, *97*
dispatch. *See* fleet management
Doll, Jeff, *30*, 131

E

earnings, annual, 31, 46, 53, 65, 71–73, 77, 101, 121, 127
Eastman, Joseph B., 18, 20
Easton, Lee, 86, *86*, 87, 98
economy
    Black Monday, 75
    Great Depression, 17–18, 19, 23
    postwar struggles, 22–23
    prosperity, 91
    recession, 46, 77, 127
    September 11 effects, 120
    2000 press release, 118–119
Educational Driving Instruction (EDI), 125–126
employees. *See also* truck drivers
    cross-training, 80–81
    hiring process, 31, 35
    mobile training centers, 125
    recruiting, 36–37, 41, 61, 64, 80
Ehrlich, Jerry, 132
The Enterpriser, 77, *77*, 78, *78*, *79*, 91, *98*

Environmental Protection Agency (EPA), 127
Epstein, Irving, 55, *55*, 68, 137
Ernst & Whinney, 75

F

Farris, J. D., 41, *41*
Federal Aid Road Act, 17
Federal Highway Administration (FHWA), 99, 101, 104
Finnes, Steve, 93, 95, 124
Firestone, 59
fleet management, 42, 49–50, 116–117
Forbes, 71, 72, 78, 105
Ford, Gerald, 54
Ford trucks, *24*, 25, *27*
Fortune 500 companies, 40–41, 108
Freightliner, *26*, *34*, *35*, 38, 101, 119
French, Rod, 38, 63, 67, 131
Frey, John, 101–103, *104*
fuel
    conservation, 20
    prices, 77, 91, 92, 119, 121
    shortages, 45

G

Gagnon, Miles, 38
Gallo, Anthony, 107
Gersix, 16
GMC, *10*
    Jimmy, 20, *21*

Reliance, *13*, 14
Goodyear Tire and Rubber, 15–16, 17, 20
Goos, George, *47*
Gra-Gar, 32, 115
Griffin Pipe Products, 40
GWR Investments, *131*

H

Hammitt, Gail, *28*
Hansohn, Gene, 64–65
Haug, Dwayne, 85, 115, *115*
Hays, Lee, 40–41
headquarters (Omaha), *44, 47, 48, 51, 54, 70, 97, 111, 114*
   computer infrastructure, 53
   constructing, 45–46
   maintenance crew, 112
   trailer shop, 52
Hebe, Jim, 63, 88
Heinson, Conrad, 31, 133
Henn, Duane, 65, 87, *87*, 89, 101, 119–120
Huff, Floyd, 38

I

IBM, 93, 124
imported freight, 59
Industry Week, 57, 71, 74, 75, 77, 78
initial public offering (IPO), 67, 68, 70–72, 75, 127
insurance, 42–43, 120, 121
International Division, 108–111, 117
International Harvester, 14

Interstate Commerce Act (ICA), 19, 25
Interstate Commerce Commission (ICC), 18, 19, 54, 57

J

Japanese manufacturing firms, 74
J. B. Hunt Transport Services, 58, 71, 72, 79
Jeffery, Thomas, 16
Johnson, Jim, 95, 117, *117*, 121, 126–127, 128
Johnson, Donna, 32, 36, 37–40, 49
Journal of Commerce, 86, 107–108
just-in-time production, 74, 79

K

Kauffman, Jeffrey, 107
Keenan, John, 40
Kennedy, John, 54
Kenworth, 16, 20, 38, *60*, 63, 101, 136
Kreutztrager, Jeff, *85*

L

Lamp Ryerson Engineers, 47
Larkin, John, 72, 75, 79
Larsen, Jim, 36, 39, *39*, 40, 41, 42, 45, 59, 139
Larsen, Myrna, 139
Laughlin, Jerry, *47*

Laughlin Construction Company, 46
lean manufacturing philosophy, 74
Leathers, Derek, 108, 109, *109*, 110–111, 117
Legg, Bill, 58, 59, 69
Lincoln Highway, 17
Lockheed Martin, 119
logistics management, 113–114
log system, 42, 97
   paperless, 97–101, 104

M

Mack Brothers Company, 11–13, 16–17, 22
maintenance operations, 112, 115
Management Information Systems (MIS), 92–93, 95, 102, 115, 124
management team, 127
Maytag, 40-41, 59
Mecray, Paul, 138
Mercer, Don, *34*
Merrill Lynch Global Securities, 107
Metro Tech, 50
Mexico operations, 107–111, 113, 120
Mid-Iowa Kenworth, 38
Midlands Business Journal, 82
Moskal, Brian, 74
Motor Carrier Act of 1980 (MCA), 57–58
Motor Carrier Act of 1935, 13, 18, 19, 43

motor carrier regulatory law, 17
M. S. Carriers, 71, 108
Munson Transportation, 71

N

National Industrial Recovery Act, 18
National Park Highway, 15
National Trucking, 49
Nebraska Motor Carriers Association, 71
Nebraska State Patrol, *82*
Nebraska Trucker, 71
Nelson, Ben, *82*
Nordlund, Marty, 83, 100, *100*
North American Free Trade Agreement (NAFTA), 107–108, 110–111

O

Office of Defense Transportation (ODT), 20
Omaha Business Hall of Fame, 95
Omaha World-Herald, 57, 70, 95, 107
OmniTRACS mobile communication system, 85
Opti Connect, 93, 95

P

PACCAR Inc., 136
Packett, Patricia, 43
Palmer Tire Company, 17
Payton, Buddy, 41–42, 49
Pearl Harbor, 19-20
Persian Gulf War, 77
Peterbilt, 60, *62,* 101, 129, 136
Pierson, Dick, 121, 123, 137
Pigott, Mark, 136, *136*
Piper Marbury, 69
Puerto Rico, 111

Q

Qualcomm communication system, 79, 85, *85,* 86–88, 97, 103, 115, 120, 125
Quantel 1 system, 50, 92

R

Radio Shack, 128
railroads, 11, 16, 19
Rapid Motor Vehicles, 14, *15*
Ratekin, Randy, 49
Reagle, George, 104
Reed, Scott, 112
Refrigerated Division, 78, 81, 83
Regional Division, 78, 81, 82
regulations, 17–18, 25, 29, 54, 57
Reiser, Richard, 95, 98, 105, *105*
Reliance Motor Truck, *13,* 14
resale program, 62–63
Road Act. *See* Federal Aid Road Act
Robertson, Gail. *See* Werner-Robertson, Gail
Robertson, Scott, 59, 61
Robertson, Vince, 92
Rock Island Railroad, 40
Rogert, Don, 134, *134,* 135
Roosevelt, Franklin D., 18, 20

S

safety
  Educational Driving Instruction (EDI), 125–126
  No-Zone, 95
  program, *81,* 89
  Qualcomm system, 87
  running over hours, 18–19, 88–89, 98
  Safety Management Team, 125–126
  truck driving simulator, *96,* 119–120
Salt Lake City Utility Trailer Company, 38
Sapp, Dean, 128
satellite communication system. *See* Qualcomm communication system
Saurer Motor Trucks, *11,* 12
Schneider National, 71, 79
Scott, Russell, *28*
September 11 terrorist attacks, 120–121, 135
shareholders, 70
Sieberling, Frank, 15–16
Silvertown tires, 17
Simon Transportation, 127
Skinner Macaroni, 38, 39–40
Smith, Wilbur, *41*

Smithsonian's National Museum of American History, 125, 129, *129*
Sony, 74
Starnes, Mike, 58, 108
Steele, John, 73–74, *74*, 95, 97–98, 99, 119
stocks, 17, 68–69, 70, 72, 134–135
Straight Side tires, 17
Studebaker, 12–13
Synowicki, Bob, *105*
    acquisitions, 128
    Data Warehouse project, 123
    disaster recovery site, 96
    driver purchase program, 63–64
    as executive vice president, 95
    paperless log system, 104–105
    Qualcomm system, 87
    as vice president and CFO, 80
synthetic fluids, 62

T

Teamsters Union, 57
technology, 105, 118, 123–125, *125*, *126*
Telpner, Zaph, 30–31
temperature control division, 85
terminals. *See also* headquarters
    Allentown, Pennsylvania, 93
    Atlanta, Georgia, 77, 78
    Council Bluffs, 45
    Dallas, Texas, 73
    Denver, Colorado, 71, *68*
    disaster recovery site, 95–96, *97*
    Henderson, Colorado, *66*
    Indianapolis, Indiana, 93
    Laredo, Texas, 109, *116*, 121
    Los Angeles, California, 68, 71
    Phoenix, Arizona, 92, *99*
    Springfield, Ohio, 68, 71
Throener, Sister Patricia, 94
Timmerman, Gerald, *31*, 32, 135, 137
tires, 13, 15–17, 20, 54–55
Total Quality Management program, 91
Traffic World, 119
training centers, mobile, 125, *125*
transcontinental journeys, *10*, 15–16
transportation authority, 25–26, 37–40, 41, 49, 53, 57–58
Transport Technology Today, 101
truck drivers. *See also* safety
    communication, 29
    driver purchase program, 59, 63–64
    driver relations group, 102
    entry-level training, 120
    home-time system, 103
    mechanical abilities, 28, 30
    pay for waiting time, 83
    recruiting, 101–103
    running heavy, 41
    shortages, 20, 71–72, 86, 107
    wages, 30, 102
truck purchasing
    buybacks, 63
    first major purchase, *34*
    one-for-two practice, 27–28
    used truck operation, 58, 63, 120–121
trucks, *51*, *56*, *57*, *61*, *72*, *76*, *80*, *102*
    comfort, 13, 28–29, 64, 103, 112
    early, 11–15
    quality, 28, 62

U

Universal Rim, 17

V

Value Added Services, 112, 113, *113*
van division, 38, 39, 41, 42

W

Wabash National Trailers, 85, 132
Wall Street, 68, 70, 119, 126, 128
Wall Street Journal, 53
Ward La France, 11
Weller, George, 86
Wellington Management, 138

INDEX

Welton, Guy, 80, 81, 115, 116, *116*, 117, 118, 132
Werner Canada, 109–110, *110*
Werner, Clarence "C. L.", *25, 34, 47, 62, 64, 69, 73, 94, 122,* 123, *130, 136*
   birth, 13, 23
   business tactics, 30–31, 36, 40, 53, 54, 60
   childhood, 23
   company philosophy, 31
   first airplane, 47, 53
   first terminal, 40
   first truck, *24,* 25, 27
   relationship with vendors, 63
   St. John's religious education center, 94
   views of his children, 128, 130–131
Werner, Clint, *130*
Werner, Curt, *33, 64, 69, 132*
   birth, 27
   Dedicated Division, 100
   earliest duties, 32–33
   Mexico operations, 107
   safety program, 89
   vice chairman of corporate development, 95
Werner, Gary, *33, 64, 69,* 118, *133*
   birth, 26
   Dedicated Division, 100
   earliest duties, 32
   investor relations, 68–69
   president, 60
   Quantel 1 system, 92
   steps down as president, 103
   vice chairman, 80
Werner, Gloria, 25
Werner, Greg, *33, 64, 69, 130, 133*
   birth, 26
   Chief Operating Officer, 117
   Dedicated Division, 100
   executive vice president, 95
   Gra-Gar, 32, 115
   Management Information Systems, 92, 93
   president, 103, 105
   sales, 53
   vice president, 60
Werner, Hugo, 23, 94, 137
Werner, Louise, 23, 94
Werner Aire, 61
Werner aviation, 53, 60–61, *74*
Werner-Bennett, Lois, 94
Werner company store, 77
Werner de Mexico, 108, 109–110, *110*
Werner International. *See* International Division
Werner Museum, 37, 92
Werner-Robertson, Gail, 32–33, *33,* 46, 50, 53, *69,* 131, *131,* 132
White Company, 14, *14*
Wickersham, Gale, 35, 131, 132
Williams, Larry, 82, 113, *113,* 114, 133
William T. Joyce Company, 29
Wilson, Arnaud J., 75
Wingfoot Express, 12, 15–16, 17
Witherell, Sue, 123, 132
World War I, 16, 20
World War II, 20, 22–23

Z

Zacks Investment Research, 121